If Life Is a Game, How Come I'm Not Having Fun?

SUNY series in Communication Studies
Dudley D. Cahn, editor

If Life Is a Game, How Come I'm Not Having Fun?

A Guide to Life's Challenges

Paul Brenner

Foreword by Carl Hosticka

STATE UNIVERSITY OF NEW YORK PRESS

Cover photo: Christopher Briscoe

Published by
State University of New York Press, Albany

© 2001 State University of New York

All rights reserved

Printed in the United States of America

No part of this book may be used or reproduced in any manner whatsoever
without written permission. No part of this book may be stored in a retrieval system
or transmitted in any form or by any means including electronic, electrostatic,
magnetic tape, mechanical, photocopying, recording, or otherwise
without the prior permission in writing of the publisher.

For information, address State University of New York Press,
90 State Street, Suite 700, Albany, NY 12207

Production by Kristin Milavec and Judith Block
Marketing by Dana E. Yanulavich

Library of Congress Cataloging-in-Publication Data

Brenner, Paul
    If life is a game, how come I'm not having fun? : a guide to life's challenges / Paul Brenner ; foreword by Carl Hosticka.
      p. cm. — (SUNY series in communication series)
    Includes bibliographical references.
    ISBN 0-7914-4963-7 (alk. paper) — ISBN 0-7914-4964-5 (pbk. : alk. paper)
    1. Play—Psychological aspects. 2. Games—Psychological aspects. 3. Conduct of life. I. Title. II. Series.

BF717.B74 2001
158—dc21
                                    00-044531

10 9 8 7 6 5 4 3 2 1

*To my parents, my great-aunt Dr. Cecile Wechsler,
and my beloved wife Priya*

A great philosopher and I, while walking one day, discovered the Ultimate Truth, the meaning and purpose of life. The meaning of life is to live, and the purpose of living is to love. Without love, life is mere existential coping. But of love, I had no clue.

Three years ago I prayed for guidance, for wisdom, for love, and what I got was a two-year spiritual sabbatical, a walking meditation in which I provided God the time and space in which to transform me, mind, body and spirit. And miracles have and continue to occur on a regular basis. You, my dear friends, I consider to be one of those miracles.

This great philosopher and I, while walking and talking, also determined that those who were loved early on, were blessed with the security of a healthy self-esteem, which allowed them to go forth into this world with less fear, open to and more willing to love. And with love, all things are possible, as love is God, and when one is loving, one is living, one is truly alive.

Thank you, for all that you have done for us, the great food, the beach, companionship, but most importantly the love.

May God continue to bless you, all the days of your life.

—Louie Rochon, *Dedication to Paul Brenner*, 25 July 1998

Contents

Foreword, Carl Hosticka   xiii
Acknowledgments   xv

Introduction   1

Part 1: Life by the Rules

1 What Life Is in the Modern Era   9

   The Elks of Sporthaven, 10
   The World as a Stage, 11
   Bob Hope and the Knights of St. Gregory the Great
       with Star, 12
   Mirna, the Queen of Azaleas, 14
   Daily Living through Role-Play, 16
   A Vitamin Called "Viewing Life as a Game," 17
   Childhood Memories, 19

2 The Parallel Worlds We Live In   23

   Private Dominions, 25
   The Religion Game, 27
   The Social Aspect of Religion, 31
   The Line between Belief and Make-Believe, 32

3 Persona and Performance   35

   The Meaning of Life for War Prisoners, 38
   Robert Landy's Role Categories in Everyday Life, 40
   Our Analog "I," 42

4 The Theatres of Society   47
   Rules of Games, 50
   Play Smart—Choose the Right Theatre, 52
   Twenty Political and Two Business Roles, 55

5 Think, Don't Believe   59
   A Game Called "Advertising," 63
   The Game Alcoholics Play, 64
   The Drama of Suffering, 66
   Play in Sickness, 67

            Part 2: Success Redefined

6 Can Work Be Playful?   73
   Games of Strategy, 74
   The Multimillion-Dollar Executive Games of
      Virtual Reality, 76
   Vacationing on the Austrian Alps, 78
   Let's Play Sisters, 80
   A Historical Snapshot of Our Paradigm, 82
   Four Chords of Mental Health, 84

7 A Journey's Aim   85
   A Conversation with Nisragadatta, 87
   The Inmates' Revolt, 90
   In the Royal Gardens of Innsbruck, 91
   The Competitive Edge, 93
   Kohn's Case against Competition, 95
   The Meaning of Anxiety, 96

8 Happiness and Bargains   99
   Successful Executives Pay the Price, 103
   Kant and the Morality of Unhappiness, 105
   How "Success in Life" May Be Redefined, 106
   Martin, 107
   How It Came to Be That We Have Ten
      Commandments, 109
   Stretching Up Hands into the Mist, 112

Contents xi

Part 3: Joyous Minds

9 The War Games Nations Play 117
  A Game Bigger than Life, 120
  Elements of Adventure, 125
  In the Armed Forces, 126
  On the Theory That We Are Genetically Evil, 127
  On the Theory That We Are Born Tabula Rasa, 128
  On the Theory That We Are Genetically Both Good
    and Evil, 129
  Lessons from the Holocaust, 130
  The Elephant and the Fly, 132
  Riding the Roller Coaster, 133

10 Peace Dance in the Moonlight 135
  Alexander's Ideal: A World United in Peace, 138
  The Game of a City of Happy People, 138
  The Inside of a Cup, 141

11 Theories of Play and Healing: Reviewing Research 143
  Five Classical Theories of Play, 144
  J. C. Friedrich von Schiller, 145
  Five Contemporary Theories of Play, 146
  Pleasure versus Utility, 147
  Prof. Lewis Terman and the Famous "Termites," 148
  Play Therapy and Healing, 148
  Role-Play and Creativity, 150
  The Perils of Illusion in Play, 151
  Animals at Play, 152

12 Life Is Tough, Tough But Fun 155
Epilogue 159
Notes 161
Bibliography 171

Foreword

For most of us, trying to make sense out of the incessant onslaught of daily life is a bewildering task. We spend most of our energies just coping with demands or trying to live up to the expectations of others. When we do get a chance to rest, we are often too exhausted to reflect on the meaning of all of our activity or to determine whether we find life satisfying or joyful.

Paul Brenner offers an interesting perspective that can help us navigate our way through this dilemma. In this well-written book, he explores the notion of games and play as metaphors for life. Rather than provide answers, Brenner allows his readers to think for themselves, to complete an idea, or to respond to a provocation. Although each of us must find our own path, Brenner helps us survey the landscape and identify the signs we meet along the way.

Is life a game? Furthermore, is "fun" the basic criteria for a "good life"?

Games usually have rules and roles. Different players contribute to the outcome in different ways, each being essential to success. The whole process only makes sense within a framework of boundaries and objectives. Contrast this to the "anything goes" nature of war, in which attaining the objective overrides all other considerations, be they fairness, fun, skill, or decency. Actually, war has become so destructive that military confrontations now resemble games since they're limited by rules and missions.

Economists and political scientists argue that the best way to understand modern society is through a "game" perspective in which individual players pursue their objectives in an atmosphere of competition with the goal of winning. Academics spend a lot of time trying to discover the "rules" of these games and to describe how they can be played more effectively.

We need to understand social action in terms of systems processes with their own unwritten rules. Each individual element contributes its own part and may do so in complete ignorance of the processes that create the whole, for example, the concept of evolution can describe the dynamics of the biosphere in terms of a few simple rules that govern the interaction of myriads of seemingly independent entities. While each individual organism views existence as a struggle with grim consequences for the weak or the slow, the development of the whole proceeds in a beautifully elegant manner.

Whether or not life is a game, there is much to be said about living life in a playful manner. The chief distinction between play and work seems to be that work is what we do for the sake of something else, while play is what we do for its own sake. Boaters tell of the famous exchange between a power boater and a sailor:

Power Boater: "Your sailboats are just too slow. When I am on my boat, I want to go fast and get someplace."

Sailor: "You just don't get it. When I'm on my boat, I am someplace."

So is life a journey or a game? Where are we going? How will we know when we get there? Brenner helps us each look at our own answers to such questions.

CARL HOSTICKA

Acknowledgments

I am privileged to have known the following people, to whom I owe a debt of gratitude for their feedback and support while I wrote this book. I gratefully thank Priscilla Ross, Kristin Milavec and Dana Yanulavich at State University of New York Press for their labor and continuous effort. I am grateful for the valuable input from Dr. Carl Hosticka and for his willingness to write the foreword to this book, and to Judy Ruiz-Compton, my creative-writing mentor. I appreciate the support and helpful comments from Charlene Phipps at the University of Oregon, Dr. Cecile Wechsler, Bill Mucklow, Toni Gose-Mucklow, Guy Peterson, David Larson, Betty Franklin, and Phyllis Thaller. Lastly, I wish to acknowledge my wife Priya for years of unfailing assistance with my research, computer work and editing suggestions, and for being a loyal sounding board for my thoughts and evolving ideas, which many married and published scholars can appreciate.

Grateful acknowledgment is made to Ron J. Flemming for permission to reprint excerpts of the poems "The Plight of Man," "New Year," and "Colors of a Rainbow" from *Heartbeats: A Book of Wisdom*, copyright 1994 by Ron J. Flemming.

Introduction

> *Play was once looked upon as a curious and unimportant feature of child life. Now it is considered a factor in education and a very important one. With this change of viewpoint has come a change in the definition of play, which now encompasses a wider range of activities. At first only aimless activities were classed as play.... The modern concept of play allows the presence of the play spirit even in work.*
>
> —Allen V. Sapora and Elmer D. Mitchell, *The Theory of Play and Recreation*

When I sent an early draft of this book to my friends for comments, one of them asked me: Where is Paul Brenner in it? Indeed I was absent from the narrative of my ideas, because I wasn't sure who I was. The next morning I began to ask the questions: Am I an economist? A writer? An individual who still plays male roles in a society that is becoming feminine and where the game-rules are changing? One morning a person wakes up, looks in the mirror, and realizes: I don't know anymore who I am. I omitted my living experience, the human story, because I was unable to recognize that I am a different person to different people—none of which I *really* am.

Following the publication of my novel *Dear Brotherhood: A Fantasy*, I received letters and telephone calls from readers with diverse backgrounds, expressing interest in my insinuated suggestion that our daily plights may be carried out as if they are games that we play with ourselves and with each other.

These inquiries prompted extensive research, which ultimately marshaled me to an important and pertinent predicament: Why are so many of us still not happy, individually and collectively? That intrigued me.

Two particular questions began to nag me: Can we as a society treat everything as a game; can we intertwine play with business, play with relationships, play with war, play with religion, and so forth? And what would be the consequences?

I began to wonder: Would a spirit of play in all aspects of everyday life become socially accepted? I felt that such an attitude ought to be a collective phenomenon in order for individuals to play it out effectively.

I began to examine the roles we play in society, and the games we enact in our lives consciously and unconsciously. I wasn't interested in the conventional viewpoint that regards us as economic resources in a race for financial prosperity. I wanted to know how much of what we do, as *feeling* individuals, is motivated by our need to succeed in a battle for *psychological survival*, since the human story always takes place in the context of other human beings.

I also wanted to know how much of what we do in the name of business and other serious affairs are in actuality suppressed games. I decided to explore the meaning of play. Intuitively I felt that play must be a natural human activity and a fundamental need for people.

I was surprised to find out, in the course of my research, how many people actually do treat life with a spirit of play. During the last three years, my understanding of the theme has evolved and deepened considerably.

As often may be the case, my attraction to this topic is embedded in my personal chronicle. I was born in Poland under Soviet occupation two years after World War II. My father was a teenager when the war broke out. He jointed the Polish underground as a young Jewish resistance fighter, fought for almost five years, was severely wounded shortly before the end of the war, and became a decorated hero. My mother was nineteen years old when I was born, shy, exceptionally beautiful, and a devout lover of good literature.

They moved to Israel when I was three. The new state was only two years old, and hundreds of thousands of homeless Jewish Holocaust survivors emigrated there from all over Europe at the same time that we did. Tiny and poor, Israel lacked the infrastructure needed to accommodate such an influx of diverse people. It took almost two decades, characterized by struggle and scarcity, food rationing, and work shortages, until everyone settled.

My parents' basic worldview became deeply ingrained early in my young and tender psyche, and underlay my activities during much of my adult life. In their experience, human beings were selfish and self-serving, and therefore no one was safe. "Life isn't a game," my mother would say. "To prevail, you must take everything seriously." Her worldview stressed insecurity, force, and survival. Thomas Hobbes, the seventeenth-century English philosopher, described it as a state of war.[1]

Be smart, watch your back, trust no one, she advised me. People are emotional and don't need a valid reason to hurt or kill others. Even one's home is no longer a castle. And don't be a romantic optimist, she added. The romantics are society's victims and fools. The ideals of love and happiness have been selling books and films because they represent a longing, not a reality. My mother still maintains that, only now she often adds: "What can I do?" with a weary smile, shrugging her haggard shoulders.

My mother is a nurse. Whenever the surrounding Arab states attacked Israel, she volunteered to help on the front line. The first time she volunteered was during the Sinai War in 1956. The second time she did it was during the Six-Days-War in 1967, when I was also on the battlefield. And when she was forty-five, she volunteered for the third time, during the Yom-Kippur War in 1973, this time with my younger brother. I was already at Rutgers University in New Jersey, studying for my MBA.

The wars, and Israel's economic woes, drove many Jewish families to immigrate again, this time to the United States. My parents refused nonetheless:

"Israel is our real home," my mother exclaimed. "Here, at least, Jews are safe from hate-crimes and persecutions. Whenever our time to die arrives, we die here."

For my parents, the Holocaust never ended.

I had to take life very seriously. I had no choice. To respect my mother's wishes I became an economist instead of a playwright or an actor. And naturally, there was no campus life for me; I was a very serious student. Afterward, I was a very serious executive. I worked long hours for multinational corporations, with an executive ulcer at the age of twenty-seven, and a divorce at thirty-one. I'm a textbook self-made successful survivor. After my ulcer exploded, my doctors predicted that I would live no longer than five more years—I didn't play much for fun, and I took nothing lightly. In my case, fatal heart failure or a recurring ulcer appeared to be an inevitable certainty in the doctors' perception. Although life grew increasingly complex and demanding, I persevered. By the time I turned forty, I yearned to break free, to be more spontaneous.

Today I believe that it isn't enough to merely persevere, day after day, only because we happen to be alive. It seems to me that we all need to enjoy the process more than just to survive it. That is why the question, what constitutes a good life, indeed keeps reemerging and continues to be an unresolved query for so many of us.

Art historians assert that the original paintings found in ancient caves were created by individuals who needed to escape from reality into fantasies, to forget for brief pauses their harsh and bothersome conditions. The Romans built entire coliseums to provide for the masses a diversion from the stresses of life. Theaters, circuses, and clowns developed as a result. The latest, an American contribution, are the movie theaters.

Amusement fields began in seventeenth-century France as pleasure gardens. They were parks interlaced with fountains, flower beds, tree-lined paths for strolling, coffeehouses—later inns and taverns in England—and a large array of sports and circus activities including tightrope, trapeze, and parachuting. When dance halls were added, dancing spread as a newly accepted form of play. There was no admission charge to these amusement gardens.

Drama goes further back. It began as a religious ritual, not as entertainment and led to comedy and humor. Much later, the clowns emerged because they made the populace laugh. From the fourteenth century hence, Europe's aristocrats regularly kept court jesters to entertain their guests, and to bring merriment to the lives of their families amid the burden and responsibility of looking after the needs of their masses.

Most towns had village fools and cared for them, because they were important to the well-being of simple folk. They made them laugh and healed their psychological wounds. The fools were so popular that they were often included in folk plays as well as in official celebrations.

Its healing power practically forced comic drama into our culture. In the solemn nativity plays, the Christ child began to be visited by clownish, foolish shepherds who would sometimes steal a sheep and hide it in the baby's cradle to make the audience laugh. Joseph started to be depicted deliberately as a simpleton, and deformed devils and dwarfs emerged as the leading clowning themes in Europe.

A major accomplishment of the American human rights movement in the early part of the twentieth century was the creation of leisure time for workers, and the awareness of dedicating this free time to fun activities. Sapora and Mitchell describe how, at the beginning of the century, piles of play sand were placed in the yard of settlement houses in Boston, while today playgrounds are considered a vital ingredient of every community planning. Recreation programs, originally intended for a couple of months during the summer, now cover the entire year. Fun initially consisted of a few simple games. Now it includes music, crafts, camps, nature study, gardening, health clubs, membership in social organizations, and many other serious activities that once were considered only the domain of school and work.[2]

The question needs to be asked: Why do we have to wait until we are done with work in order to play? Why can't we incorporate it into all everyday activities—into our work, study, buying, selling, love, marriage, divorce, and so forth—without compromising the quality and import of these pursuits?

We consume too much alcohol, nicotine, and drugs, eat too much, overindulge in sex, and buy too many things we don't need, only because we suffer from too much anxiety and stress. It is apparent that our play activities in the evenings and on the weekends do not balance the stress accumulated during our working hours. We now hear voices that advocate a shift to a four-day workweek. In our cultural context, I sincerely doubt that it would accomplish anything more than increased violence and crime.

An alternative solution seems to be the intertwining of serious endeavors with play, the infusion of business and work with a playful spirit. In other words, to treat all things as if they are games rather than dead-serious projects, matters of life-and-death. When I speak in this book about play, I refer to the serious things that we do all day merely infused with a playful spirit.

There are advantages in regarding play as an attitude, according to the social psychologist Susanna Millar. She suggests that play cannot be defined as a particular kind of activity, with characteristics that distinguish it from other activities. Rather, it is the mood of the person regardless of what she or he is doing.[3]

I found in my research ample scientific evidence indicating that a lighter attitude toward life may prove to be much healthier for us as individuals, and hence for our society. Yet, in spite of the growing number of studies that exist in support of a playful bearing toward everyday activities, the widespread tendency is still to take ourselves, everything we do and say, even our games, extremely seriously.

A great deal of attention has been given to diet, fitness, aerobics, meditation, and fun excursions. Little consideration has been given to the advantages of a playful attitude toward life in general, taking ourselves less severely, treating serious matters gamefully, and designating all our pursuits—not only mindless entertainment and some fun activities—as games that we play.

That's what this book is about.

The book is endowed with quotations from scientists and profound thinkers—psychologists, anthropologists, sociologists, philosophers, theologians, and historians who delineate the benefits of applying the spirit of play to everyday life.

Researching and writing this book has been a labor of love for me. I hope that my undertaking has been successful, that I have been able to interest you with the idea that our human dramas may be consciously played as games. If we play life, existence can become an aggrandized joy for many more of us.

Part 1

Life by the Rules

To live life as a game is to have a life of adventure that surpasses all description. . . . What happens to the child in play can happen to the adult. And when it does, paradise is present.

—Robert E. Neale (psychiatrist)

1

What Life Is in the Modern Era

This life is a game proceeding before us.
—Gandhi, *Interpretation of the Bhagvadgita*

"Life is one big dress-up," says Muffy VanderBear. For those who aren't familiar with the VanderBears, they are professedly the best-dressed teddy bears in the American stuffed animal kingdom. For my wife Priya, a psychologist, and for her mother, Phyllis—who devoutly collect, dress, and nurture the VanderBear family—life is a conscious medium for play.

At the beginning of the eighteenth century, the Catholic Church dominated European education and schools, and strict measures were enforced to ban all forms of play and humor. The church issued the following decree:

> We prohibit play in the strongest terms. The students shall rise at five o'clock in the morning, summer and winter. The students shall be indulged with nothing which the world calls play. Children shall be instructed in this matter in such a way as to show them, through the presentation of religious principles, the

wastefulness and folly of all play. The reward of those who seek earthly things is tears and sorrow.[1]

For many people in the Christian world, existence—including play—evolved as a somber and rueful business, as the following story vividly illustrates:

The Elks of Sporthaven

On a foggy Saturday afternoon in March of 1998, the Benevolent Protective Order of Elks chapter in the little fishing town Sporthaven, Oregon, inaugurated new officers. In a colorful ceremony, fifty-five-year-old Phil, a local merchant, became the new exalted ruler. Stocky and proud, wearing a jeweled coronet, Phil stood under the crossed swords, with large medals hanging from his necklace, gold-rimmed glasses, and a modern bow tie, and received the "royal gavel" with serious eyes and a tight-lipped smile.

The new officers were mostly local vendors. Queuing up in their rented attire, they placed their left hands over their chests, raised their right hands, and solemnly swore to take their new stations in the organization. They were presented with jewelry that represented their new positions.

The chairperson of the board reported the end of a good year. The funds continued to roll in, he said, and new people were joining. Rod, the head of the bingo games, was proclaimed "Elk of the Year."

Over a cup of coffee, I reviewed the faces of the players on the front page of the morning newspaper. The photographs taken at the Elks ceremony revealed tension and anxiety, not fun. The tame smile didn't hide Phil's heavy burden from the cameras: I promise to serve our society; I will do everything to maintain Rod's precedence in the Bingo program.

Phil, Rod, and their friends became Elks probably to create a balance in their lives by adding play. Now they will need a vacation to get away from it. Phil will ski, and Rod will play tennis. But all of the activities today are competitive and assiduous, and gone again is the sought balance between work and play. Strain, not release and fun, permeates both.

The Elks ceremony serves as a simple illustration of the contention made by the psychiatrist Adam Blatner and his wife that a good deal of what we call "culture" is based on play activities; that one of the most obvious things about people is that they play.[2] Whenever we interact, we play a game with each other. Only we do not treat that as play. Observed closely, our ceremonies and rituals, and the socioeconomic and political activities of our numerous clubs and organizations, are games humans play. Although taken seriously, these games are not motivated by a need for physical survival, but by a basic instinct to play.

We play to add stimulation and meaning to everyday activities.

In fiction and in games paupers can become rulers, placing a crown on their heads and a gavel in their hands. In a democracy, unless it is play, people—whether they are middle class or elite—do not become royalty and knights.

In play, our boundless imagination can be expressed and manifested. This is noble, for within each of us there is an undeniable demand for joy. But as soon as we take the game too seriously, it translates into an obligation, and that usually robs the activity of its fun, merriment, and joy.

The World as a Stage

The world is a stage, and every man and woman is an actor.

—Shakespeare, *As You Like It*

William Shakespeare's celebrated message is repeated in all of his plays. In one great text after another he labors to show how all men and women act out the scripts of their roles and destinies in the theater of life, most of the time consciously, sometimes unconsciously.

Shakespeare's famous view of life as play is not unique to him. The great American essayist and poet, Ralph Waldo Emerson, echoed Shakespeare's attitude. As a practicing Unitarian minister he liked to preach, and as a prolific writer and lecturer he dominated the literary society in New England for more than thirty years. In one of his most quoted adages he describes the human environment as a spectacle. He tells us: Observe the passersby—as you ride in a coach, they look like a fleeting puppet show.

Plotinus taught neo-Platonic philosophy in the third century and was a profound Roman thinker. He treated all realms of daily life—political, economic, religious, military, sex, even crime—as theatrical episodes. Together, he said, they form the single grand performance of life:

> If in form the world resembles an organism, all that happens in the world is comparable to a drama on stage. Death is a change of roles. The conflicts among individuals indicate that everything in human life is a game. As on a stage, we must consider the murders, the different kinds of deaths, the conquest and pillage of cities, all as mere changes of scenes.[3]

We can imagine Plotinus lecturing to his students: Everything, including grief and lamentation, are acts of a plot.[4]

Bob Hope and the Knights of St. Gregory the Great with Star

> *The comic perspective on human existence is particularly close at hand in this play world of sociability.*
>
> —Peter L. Berger, *The Precarious Vision*

To fully grasp the theatrical character of human society, as a large dramatic production, let us look at another picture in our collective photo album:

It was Wednesday, 10 June 1998, in Los Angeles. The Catholic Church honored Bob Hope for his financial contributions. The famous film star and his wife Dolores were inducted into the Order of St. Gregory the Great with Star (what a designation!), one of the highest papal knighthoods (what a title!). Eighty-nine-year-old Dolores became the third female knight in St. Gregory's Order, and Bob, at the age of ninety-five, became the seventh male member of the society's chapter in Los Angeles, during a lavish costume party orchestrated by the cardinal.

Similar awards, honors, and ceremonies take place in various organizations and communities every day. They are carnivals of masks and dramatized games that mark the playful aspect of our societies. They could serve as a wonderful source of fun, were they not approached as merely political, social, or economic functions. However, it is politically correct to believe that responsible adults must always be serious, especially about what we consider important things.

Educators and philosophers like to remind us that we are social animals. We live in a community with others rather than in isolation. Consequently we depend on each other for everything. Psychologically we exist for, and find meaning for our lives in, the activities and customs of the large groups we belong to.

A society is like a puzzle board. Every individual is an interlocking piece that somehow fits on the board. We are kept in place by the other pieces that surround us. We are born into a society and we cannot live independently of it, be it conceptually, practically, or emotionally. Our lives without a society is inconceivable to us. We can fantasize about it, but it wouldn't be a reality. And as all the interlocking pieces fit on the puzzle board, society is not about love. We are in it not because we love human beings. I doubt that most of us do. Unconditional love exists only in isolation where there are no other human beings but oneself. It does not even exist in monasteries and ashrams, as those like myself who have spent time in them have found out. It is difficult to love the human species. The nicest-sounding commandment, yet the most nonsensical, is to love others as ourselves. I am more compassionate and accepting toward my neighbors than I am toward myself. With myself I am as I *really* am, a tamed beast.

But I am a social beast. I exist not only *in* society, but *for* society. I live for the drama I create in the groups I belong to, for the impressions I manage to produce on others, and for the attention I manage to generate from other pieces in the puzzle. I would gladly die today if I only knew I could stay around to watch the impact that my death spawns around me.

As human beings, everything we do, every decision and desire we generate, is triggered and shaped by how other humans would respond, approve, or disapprove. We are so conditioned to tune into the will and wishes of society that not only are the feelings and opinions of our immediate family and friends crucial to us, but also the impression we make on complete strangers we cross in the streets.

We are entertainers. We garb ourselves; some of us paint their hair in purple and green, or drill holes in their ears and lips and noses. We give each other medals and titles and beautifully packaged greeting cards and gifts. Some of us go to great lengths to organize parties, dinners, and social clubs, where we can wear costumes and make an effort to impress people. Afterward we go home and recharge the reservoir of energy that got drained in being polite, amicable, and loving.

My father once said that if I live long enough, I will reach the stage in which *nothing* will ever surprise me. I must have arrived at that phase. Life lost its hold over me. When it no longer has a grip over us, when it no longer scares or intimidates us, we begin to do things because we are compelled to do them.

However, we convince ourselves that everything we do is important in order to make everything we do, and everything that happens to us, count for something. In his remarkable book, *A Philosophy of Play*, Dr. Luther Halsey Gulick offers an excellent example. A father comes home from work and finds his nine-year-old daughter busy writing something. Her face and hand movements clearly indicated great concentration and extreme tension:

"What are you doing?" He asks his little girl.

"Please don't disturb me," she replies without lifting her head. "I'm doing something very important. I'm on the entertainment committee of the Saturday Afternoon Club, and I'm writing the program."[5]

Contemporary educators increasingly believe that viewing life with humor, embracing ourselves and our society much less solemnly than we presently do, may be a possible road to happiness and cooperation.

Our daily lives may be "fought" as though we live on a battlefield, or enacted as a game. Even a game, when conducted as a matter of life-and-death, is no longer a "game"; it is a battle that turns the game, and life, into a struggle and conflict. Conversely, when winning a war becomes secondary to the experience of adventure, it can indeed become a game. As the sociologist Peter Berger reminds us, taking our costume parties too seriously means, by its very nature, missing an essential aspect of our political reality.[6]

Mirna, the Queen of Azaleas

The more profound double sense of "social game" is that not only the game is played in a society as its external medium, but that, with its help, people actually play society.

—Georg Simmel (famed German sociologist)

The small seaside town where we used to reside provides many examples of social drama. About 5,500 people live there, many fishermen and a handful of merchants and civil servants.

Once a year, in May, the community is celebrating an Azalea Festival. It is the central event of the year. High school girls compete for the title of Azalea Queen. Tension mounts as the date gets nearer:

"I'm excited, and ready to represent the community," said Robin, one of the five finalists in 1998, to the local media. "I grew up in this town, and the Azalea princesses were my role models. Now I'm a role model for other girls."

The young Azalea "princesses" take this role seriously.

In a personal interview, the board of judges told each contestant:

"You have just been hired by a leading TV station. Your job is to sell a service or product. Pick a product or service and sell it to us now."

Princess A decides that she wants to sell computers to the judges. Another markets aerobics. Princess C chooses to be the public relations agent for the local chamber of commerce. The fourth offers a particular toothpaste. And the future queen fancies the role of a salesperson for a hair-growing product. Naturally, these were the young princesses' unbiased ideas.

The coronation of the queen takes place about a month before the festival. In a precisely detailed ceremony, the princesses walk down the aisle escorted by formally uniformed Coast Guardsmen, awaiting with anxiety the announcement of the winner. Mirna, a lovely blond, daughter of a local dentist, bursts into tears as her name is proclaimed. She has just become the Azalea queen, and the local crowd cheers enthusiastically. She wipes her tears of joy with her white-gloved hands; then, escorted by her prosperous and proud father, she waves Elizabeth-like.[7]

"Within the social drama one is given the opportunity to stretch beyond one's expected parameters,"[8] says Dr. Robert Landy.

Landy is a drama therapist and a professor of psychotherapy at New York University. He believes that social drama is the foundation on which human society functions, and the source of all of the roles that we play as individual members and as communities. Role-play, rituals, costumes, and masks are essential components of our social drama. Also of human play.

Daily Living through Role-Play

Our way of life resembles a fair. The greater part of the crowd comes to buy and sell, and a few come only to look. Know all of you, who are busied with land, slaves and public posts, that these are nothing but fodder for a comedian's routine.

—Epictetus (popular Roman philosopher and freed slave)

Playing life takes many forms. There is hardly a moment in which we do not play some sort of role. We continually dramatize characters in order to fulfill duties. Much of the time we perform for others—we are, for each other, both accomplices and audience. And sometimes we are our own audience. Whether a writer or a businessperson, rich or homeless, famous or anonymous, we play parts in the grand theater of life. And in each role that we perform, we enact a script that we have learned from our society in the course of the ongoing training that make us civilized human beings. As we mature into adulthood, our culture and environment provide us with manuscripts and shape the roles that we continue to perform for the rest of our lives. We become actors. And when this process becomes unconscious and automatic, when we no longer think about it, the role we play no longer feels like a personification but as an identity.

And yet, when I speak to an audience I perform the role of a speaker, a sage, or an expert. I don't mumble, I choose my words carefully, I coax the audience to think—so much, but not too much—I don't sprawl in the chair, and I make hand and facial gestures to imitate enthusiasm. I deliberately stage a persona. I act the character that I wish to present.

Many of us recognize that practically everything we do is a performance. Most of the time we are conscious of the particular characters we wish to present. Even when we are not fully aware of our dramatization—mostly in intimate circumstances—a part deep within our being still knows that we are acting. We do it because that is how our society functions.

I sport the part of a husband when I am with my wife, and when I talk about her even if she is absent. Suppose I didn't want to impersonate a spouse but rather *be* it, I wouldn't know what this means. I'm familiar with the contents of this role, all that it entails, simply because my environment taught me. It has become one of my personas, one of the masks that I wear regularly.

Similarly, I portray a neighbor, a salesperson, a consumer, a voter, and an author. I know how to act these parts because I'm civilized; I practiced a hundred scripts. I'm never out of a role; I always present myself in some way, even when I'm alone. By becoming a conscious actor I can be a better role-player, which helps me become more *productive*, more *efficient*, more *creative*, and have more fun in the process. Not a bad payoff.

A Vitamin Called "Viewing Life as a Game"

> *Play should interest our contemporary world more than perhaps it does. Not only in the United States, but all over the world, man is much concerned with freedom, activity for its own sake. . . . Today, however, we seldom associate freedom with play. Freedom is grim, something to be fought for . . . instead of generating effusiveness, spontaneity and joy.*
>
> —Walter J. Ong

My great-aunt Cecile is a ninety-two-year-old physician, a strong, gray-haired little lady who still, at her age, practices family medicine in New York City. She objects to my game theory of life. She said to me:

"It is very sad that we must take our lives so seriously, but what can we do? Existence, after all, is very hard. Every day is a new fight. The game theory empties our struggles of any real meaning; it turns our suffering into a pathetic experience."

I believe the contrary. I believe that the game theory gives our struggles a new meaning and fills them with fun. Echoing the Buddha, my great-aunt Cecile recognizes the fact that suffering is inevitable. It saddens her, but she finds no solution for it:

"I fear," she added, "that people will misinterpret your message. They will think that everything is a 'big joke' to you."

"You've told me that the world is so beautiful. It's true," I replied. "You tell me that the world is a magnificent adventure. You tell me that this world is a unique creation, perhaps one of a kind. But, you tell me, it cannot be a happy place?"

The idea that the world is not, perhaps cannot be, a happy place, is a hard one for me to swallow, in spite of the harsh facts of reality: "Life must be lived as play,"[9] Plato told his pupils. I cannot help thinking that Plato made a point worth exploring.

Many things in life *are* consequential, and must be taken seriously—such as holding a job, raising a family, and looking after our parents. On the other hand, when we ascribe so much import, weightiness, and anguish to our activities, even our sports games, we end up taking little joy in them.

Awhile back, I made the decision that since I play all the time anyway—we all do while forgetting that we do—I might as well enjoy it. The hitch was to stop taking my self so damn seriously, and to catch myself every time I do. When I finally stopped taking myself seriously, I became alive. And that's what this book is about, *lightening up*.

Although I do not believe that I, or anyone, can effectively instruct another "how to become alive," since it largely depends on one's psychological background, I do believe that the right attitude is a big part of it. Therefore, the idea is to inspire readers to want to lighten up, and to develop and nurture a playful attitude toward existence in general in the form that best suits one's personality and psychological makeup. It is one of those things whose consequences one does not realize until one does it.

What vitamins and minerals do for a healthy body, viewing life as a game does for a happy, sound, and productive mind. It is no wonder that play is used in therapy. Participating in life's games consciously and deliberately might yet become the mark of Western civilization.

Anne Lamott is a wonderful writer, and, I am told, a good instructor and one funny woman. In *bird by bird* she writes: "We are a species that needs and wants to understand who we are. Sheep lice do not seem to share this longing, which is one reason they write so very little."[10] Writing this book was my effort to comprehend ourselves, what we do, and why we do what we do. This work is about human life in society—what social order is, and what it does to us as individuals.

A growing number of psychiatrists and therapists now acknowledge the fact that much of our nervousness and despair is caused by the failure to reconcile life's meaninglessness. We are poorly equipped to consciously deal with the lack of any real purpose, the futility of our existence, hardships, and trials. Consequently, we give meaning to our existence through the roles we play in society, through the games we dramatize in our communities and religious institutions, and through the theologies and philosophies that we create. We take life seriously to give it a meaning, and to feel validated and safe. But in this process we deprive ourselves of the joy that "playing life" awards.

In *The Last Vampire*, Sherlock Holmes keenly reminds us that it is one thing to diagnose a problem, another to resolve it. With his brier tobacco pipe, the observant eyes of a scientist, and the mind of a philosopher, Holmes is many people's favorite detective. What does Holmes have to do with this book? Everything. To Holmes, life was a game.

The famed American educator Abraham Joshua Heschel voiced the concern that the modern person is losing the power of celebration. We seek to be amused instead of celebrating life, he said. Being entertained, to receive pleasure from an act or a spectacle initiated by others, is a passive state. Our lives do not get celebrated this way.

Years ago, I copied into my diary the following verse. Unfortunately I didn't write down its source. I wish I could take credit for these eloquent words, but I can't, and even though I am unable to acknowledge their well-deserving author, I would like to share them with you:

> Masters in the art of living draw no sharp distinction
> between their work and their play, their labor and
>   their leisure,
> their mind and their body, education and recreation.
> They simply pursue their vision through whatever
>   they are doing,
> leaving to others to determine whether they are
>   working or playing.
> To themselves, they always seem to be doing both.

Childhood Memories

My mother and father are Jewish survivors of the Holocaust. Their traumatic experiences left them with a suspicious view of humanity, and a perpetual fear of life.

In my youth I harbored an aspiration to become a playwright and an actor. I did both successfully through my junior high school years. I enrolled in a professional acting school, wrote the plays for my classes, and performed leading roles. I enjoyed acting, and rendered it well. A couple of plays produced by the drama school took me on a tour around the country. I began to talk about a career in the field. My parents, however, objected vehemently:

"Actors and writers are starving artists. To be successful in this world, you must be ready for the worst. Remember that you will be alone when troubles come, and they will."

My family always lived in expectation of adversity. To us this was the real world.

Children like to fantasize about virtual realities, because in them we can be anything we want to be. Since we did not have school buses, I walked over a mile each morning to school, and again back home every afternoon. It gave me the opportunity to daydream without being scolded that I was wasting time in an unproductive activity. I could fantasize about being a famous author or a star on Broadway. But I grew up to be a pragmatic survivalist.

After returning in one piece from the Six-Days-War, I had to relinquish my artistic ambitions and enrolled in a school of economics. I became a corporate executive, launching an insensitive, rather ruthless business career. As an adult, I forget how to be playful. I ignored the value of play, growing oblivious to the healing qualities of playfulness. Corporate greed became the name of the game, but I saw it as *survival*. I found myself extremely serious, a highly driven overachiever, and bereft.

I think that many of us take too many things too seriously, because of our desperate effort to make everything count, to make all things meaningful. And yet, we are inspired by Superwoman, James Bond, Zorro, Robin Hood, even Lex Luther. Garb and costumes are important to us. Military and police uniforms, doctor and nurses' uniforms, guards' uniforms, school uniforms, sports uniforms, and business suits and briefcases—all are costumes. Flags, ribbons, medals, and passports are accessories in the games we play with each other. They both define and remind us of the roles we enact. They guide our actions, conduct, and worldviews.

Now I am often aware of an underlying sense of unreality when I am doing something *serious* or *important,* or when I interact with individuals who take so seriously whatever it is they happen to be doing, as if the unforeseen destiny of the world, or of our lives, really depended on it.

I will leave you, for now, with the words of the acclaimed Dutch anthropologist, Johan Huizinga. I find his keen historical and philosophical insight beaming the spotlight on my work's theme:

> Our species has been named *Homo Sapiens*—"Man the Rational." Since then, we have come to realize that we are not as reasonable as the naive eighteenth-century philosophers thought. Therefore, in the modern age, the fashion is to refer to ourselves as *Homo Faber*—"Man the Maker." There is a third function—just as important as "reasoning" and "making"—and that is "playing." Next to *Homo Faber*, and perhaps on the same level as *Homo Sapiens*, "Man the Player"—*Homo Ludens*—deserves a place in our list of names.[11]

2

The Parallel Worlds We Live In

For many individuals, external reality remains, to some extent, a subjective *phenomenon.*

—D. W. Winnicott, *Playing and Reality*

When humanity started to develop the ability to think and conceptualize, they began to live in two parallel domains. One is the external world of action, movement, and enterprise; here we act, react, and interact. The second world is that of phantasms; it exists in our minds; here we conceptualize, feel, and believe.

In the first we undergo a cold and *factual* experience. In the other, we transform this experience into an emotional or *conceptualized* affair.

The inner realm is the world of imagination, intuition, passion, rationalization, and denial. Our awareness mostly dwells here, making the inner world our depicted or reasoned-out reality. Here we generate our hopes, joys, pleasures, attractions, disappointments, repulsions, and frustrations.

Our inner world turns the mathematical and ruthless facts of the external world into miracles and wonder, or it turns them into atrocities. Here we transform the ordinary events of the outer world into aspirations, fancies, and chimeras. We escape from the uncomfortable aspects of reality into the misty gardens of our inner worlds.

In the domain of our internal worlds, we have an ideal image of ourselves. How we appear to people in the outer world is rarely how we think of ourselves in the recesses of our internal domains. You and I are the *subject* of our inner realms. But in the outer, we are *objects*. The need to continually undergo a transition from being the subject to being an object is often perplexing, and the process is strenuous. At times we continue to operate and relate in the world without making that transition.

As Henry Thoreau, the American naturalist and author, said, we "see" the outer world in which we function only in our mind's eye, but we don't actually *look at* it. We create an interpretation of the outer world and of society according to how it suits our personal hopes and fears. It is not true that facts and impartial grounds determine our worldview, because you and I—even scientists, philosophers, and scholars—manipulate all the available facts, findings, and laws, to create theories that support our feelings about ourselves and about the people we affiliate with.

We live in perpetual duality. The real experience of our life is a combination of the inner and outer worlds, the outcome of their interaction. Maturity calls for recognition of this duality. The constant tension between these parallel worlds creates the dramatic quality of our daily lives.

Human temperament is not something that is readily changeable, contrary to what some self-help books suggest. Our personalities are the visible aspects of our mental and emotional landscapes. Our psychological dispositions are formed at an early age together with our approach and feelings toward our environment. We even tend to assume that we are alike. We are not. We share an external sphere of activity where we imitate each other. But we cannot easily transcend our inner worlds, our individual mind-sets.

We want to be taken care of, to be nurtured and pampered. We want to believe that society can be a place where we might feel at home.[1] That's why we create religions and metaphysical systems where we can resort to supernatural explanations and ideologies of self-sufficiency. We can manipulate the elements that make up our mental orb. But in the cradle of society we have to be interdependent and productive.

Our external world is not something that we create as individuals. Historical processes have influenced and shaped it, and these historical processes are blind to us. As individuals, we only get to interact in the outer world. To function efficiently and productively in it, we often battle against our own temperament and with what goes on in our mental worlds.

As Freud noted, a large part of our lives is an attempt to resolve conflicts between these two parallel worlds. A full resolution, he maintained, cannot be attained. Nearly all human behavior illustrates that. There's a misconception that the two worlds are reconciled through feelings. We continue to experience both worlds concurrently and without thorough conciliation. Thus, many people live out their lives in perpetual discord. Freud called it the "friction between the conscious and the unconscious," or the "friction between the individual and society."[2] We never really integrate the two worlds completely.

Most of us think that we are free and equal. However, we are neither independent nor totally free. Inequality is both natural and inevitable. We are not born with the same intellectual, emotional, or temperamental properties or with the same looks or charisma. A few lucky individuals may be happy and content even in prison. The rest of us are unhappy even when we are free and capable to roam endlessly across the planet. Freedom, happiness, and peace are also fixtures of our individual mental landscape.

Many of us like to think that we don't care if a particular element of our belief system does not make sense. If it makes sense to us, we like to hold it as *our truth*. What we actually mean is that because somehow it serves a purpose in the context of our inner world, we *wish* it to be part of our outer world as well, true or not. There exists within us an emotional need to reconcile the two worlds by hook or by crook. As Freud said, for most people the external reality never becomes fully objective.

Private Dominions

An external *consistency means that an individual's actions present a cohesive whole to the outside world.* Internal *consistency means*

> *that his actions present such a whole to himself, in terms of his ideas, emotionality and his picture of himself.*
>
> —Peter Berger, *The Precarious Vision*

The human mind has evolved in such a way that now we are, for the most part, a *walking mind,* an all-encompassing mind that has legs and hands and a face. Animals also have minds, but the minds of other species may not be as rich and active. Their span of imagination is perhaps not as varied and as far-reaching as our's has become.

I say *perhaps,* because who is to know the mind of a bird or a dog or a whale. We know that they have thoughts, that they hallucinate and dream like we do, but we don't know about what, or whether their mind is as intense, lush, vivid, and abounding as our's.

Some of us blur our inner with the outer world, assuming them to be the same, perceiving the self to be unitary in both realms. Napoleon was such a man most of his life. His ideal was to become the celebrated emperor of a unified Europe. He believed it was possible, and that most people wanted it. In the end he concluded: "imagination rules the world."[3]

As Dr. Julian Jaynes articulates, our mind is a *secret theater* of speechless monologues and anticipatory counsel; an invisible mansion of all moods, musings, and mysteries; a whole kingdom where each of us reigns reclusively alone.[4]

My friend Judy teaches writing and psychology in a community college. She once sent me the following note:

> The past in reality does not exist. Not even the moment exists when I started writing this. The past exists in my mind, but my mind is not always reliable. For example, I might remember a certain event, and I probably recall it in a certain way. But see, I've never really seen things like other people see things. I guess that's because of *my* point-of-view.
>
> Well, gee. From where I'm sitting, they looked like zebras to me. They were really referees at a basketball game, but if the light is right, and so on, they're zebras, for sure. Does everybody else get it and I don't?

Christopher is a socialist and idealist. He meets and falls in love with a wealthy woman, even though she belongs to the upper class that he hates and wishes to destroy. In spite of his love affair, he keeps promulgating and preaching his ideals about a class struggle, because it somehow gives meaning to his life in what he experiences as an irrational world.

The theory of the parallel twin worlds is important for an understanding of ourselves. We have two selves—the private self and the public self—the subjective and the objective. The external is our public world, while the inner and mental is our private world. They are parallel spheres that touch, and we shift back and forth between them. Young children move freely between the mental and the outer worlds. For adults, the cold and harsh facts of society are much more encroaching, and friction is increasingly stressful. This coexistence creates the dualistic nature of our reality, and results in our being perpetually disjointed from the external world and in disharmony in our inner world.

Here are a few illustrations: We speak of oneness, but we cannot sense or experience it; we can philosophize about connectedness, but we may neither feel nor grasp it. And we theorize about unconditionally loving each other, even though it may be the hardest and most unnatural thing for us to do. We are dependent on one another for almost everything, yet we behave as if we are independent and free agents. That's why we create a society, but we compete with each other as though we are self-sufficient entities and not an interrelated group. A look at the games and subgames we play in politics, business, philosophy, and religion further demonstrates this observation.

The Religion Game

As one generation has followed another, religion has persisted. While secularization progresses in some parts of a society, a countervailing intensification of religion goes on in other parts.

—Rodney Stark and William Sims Bainbridge,
The Future of Religion

Religions fascinate me. They award insight into our minds and shed light on our basic needs more than other human activity. I agree with Drs. Stark and Bainbridge, that the predictions that organized religion is disappearing in Western society are in error. They fail to recognize religion's dramatic nature.

In fact, Stark and Bainbridge tell us, new religions constantly continue to appear. Whether or not they make any headway largely depends on the vigor of the dominant organized religions of the day.[5]

We seek rewards, at least rewarding explanations, for the irrational hardships, failures, and pain that being alive inflicts on all of us. Religions address a fundamental void created by the meaninglessness of existence, the futility of struggle, and the senselessness in the atrocities that the human species and forces of nature commit. No one seems to be free of that need, poor and rich alike, even idealistic naturalists.

Religion is completely within the realm of our imagination—the domain of our inner worlds—and therefore under our personal control; while life's external circumstances are not. This control comforts us. "Adam Smith" says that "sometimes illusions are more comfortable than reality."[6] He is right. Logic doesn't guarantee us a peaceful night's sleep, while religious comfort may.

Furthermore, we fancy the drama.

Ritual and magic have traditionally been the central elements of theater, play, and religion. By taking a close look, we may discover the playful dimension in our religions and the religious dimension in our play. A wonderful illustration is the religious service described by the sociologist Frank E. Manning. It was, perhaps still is, a typical Sunday program at the New Testament Church of God in Bermuda:

> It begins, as most religious services of many denominations do, with songs, clapping and occasional dancing in the rear and along the aisles. In that particular church, the collection baskets are passed around quite early, and the pastor says, intentionally blunt:
>
> "Oh God, please touch their hearts, and touch their pocketbooks. We are really enjoying the blessings of the Lord, glory be to God. I trust that you have already enjoyed the Lord, and I assure you that it will get better further on."
>
> Then the pastor tells his parish how the "speeding demon" made him press on the gas pedal to drive faster than the speed limit.
>
> "It happened so fast; I didn't realize what I was doing," he said.
>
> Of course there was a speed trap, a chasing policeman, and a handsome fine. The speeding demon, an evil agent of Satan, provides a thrilling hook for the sermon. A condemnation of the

Bermudan women's custom to seductively wear short skirts may also be a good opener for the *word of God*. The pastor's tone grows angry and urgent, now he speaks about the Day of Judgment and the ever-nearing destruction of planet Earth because of the growing sin in Bermuda.

"You may be dead tomorrow!" he exclaims a blazing warning.

"Amen!" the congregation shouts. "Preach, pastor, preach! Jesus, carry him through! It's the truth!"

A drunk man happens to stagger into the church. Designated members volunteer to lead him to a front seat, and kneel beside him to keep him from falling over. The seasoned pastor seizes the moment. Pointing toward the drunkard, he addresses the flock:

"This brother wants to be delivered tonight. He wants to be loosed from the enemy. Thank you, Jesus!"

The drunk man moans and shakes, feeling sick.

"These are the signs of the struggle between Jesus and Satan over the man's soul," the pastor hammers at his audience.

The miserable man leans forward and vomits. Two volunteers run out to get sawdust to cover the spew on the floor.

"The blood of Jesus is against you, demon!" the pastor calls in frenzy. "Right now, in Jesus's name, I command you, loose your hold on this man! Come out, come out, come out. He is coming out, glory be to God! Right now the blood of Jesus prevails against you, Satan."

The congregation is pleased. They clap. They break into chanting and repeat the pastor's last words like a mantra:

"By the blood of Jesus, by the blood of Jesus, by the blood of Jesus . . . he's washed as white as snow."

The drunk man, aware of the enthusiastic response that his vomiting triggers, spews forth again.

"This is it, this is it, come out Satan," the pastor exclaims. "Hallelujah! Hallelujah!"

Some persons resume dancing in the aisle. The spirit is high at that church on that Sunday.

"We have witnessed a manifestation of the power of God here," the pastor instructs dramatically. "In my name they shall cast out devils. At least four devils came out of this brother tonight. And while the devil has gone out, the spirit of God has come in. God wants to use you, He's brought you here for a purpose, He'll make you what He desires you to be!"

Gratified, the drunkard throws up one more time and slumps over in his seat.

"Thank you Jesus. We really felt a gush of the Holy Spirit here tonight," the artful pastor quips in a humorous mood as he returns to the pulpit.[7]

Dr. Frank Manning believes that religious services act as a form of entertainment. He asked a participant:

"Why do you go to church?"

"To have a good time in the Lord," the man replied.

Indeed, rituals provide rich and absorbing entertainment. Not only religious, also political and social ceremonies, evoke strong emotional responses, just like plays, movies, and novels. They can easily provoke a violent and intense reaction when they leave their participants stranded without a resolution, stewing in strong feelings of anxiety, fear, or grief. Or, on the other hand, they may generate in their audience a deep sense of healing.

Johan Huizinga, the famed Dutch anthropologist, expressed his great surprise to the fact that so few scholars have paid attention to the element of play in religion. Rituals are "prominent areas for the appearance of the spirit of play,"[8] he says, because they contain all of the elements that are necessary to make good theater—imaginative show, dramatic performances, fabulous costumes, climactic music, and emotional stimulation. In addition, he points out, religious myths are filled with enormities, absurdities, and humor.

Dr. Frank Salamone, a contemporary anthropologist at St. John's University, shares the same perception in his essay "Religion as Play": "Religion is a game with clearly defined rules. It does indeed take people outside themselves.... In short, it is play."[9]

Conscious players know that their inner world is not all-inclusive, that alongside it exists the external world, where, in order to interact and produce, they must be efficient. Religion is part of the inner world.

According to Rodney Stark, lower-class people are more likely to pray in private, to believe in the doctrines of their faith, and to have intense religious experiences than upper-class people. However, upper and middle classes display greater religious commitment when it comes to religious affiliation, attendance, and all of the other aspects that make up ritual.[10]

It is a social game.

The Social Aspect of Religion

The adult remains on the work level for the most part, and his entries into the world of play are partial, relating only to certain aspects of life. So it is no wonder that the participant responds in terms of religion.

—Robert E. Neale, "Play and the Sacred"

Dr. Neale is an ordained minister and practicing pastor, professor of religion, and a psychiatrist. He believes that religious people simply participate in a story.[11]

A difficulty arises, he says, when a religious player takes the story seriously to the point of considering it sacred. The purpose of play is to let us relax. To the good player the contents and results of the game are secondary. But while play, religion included, can be a healthy diversion from the real world, the real world has come to be considered a diversion from religion. And, Neale says, that's how religion separated itself from real life and from being fun.[12]

I read in a number of books how the sacred tends to create tension in people. Sir James G. Frazer believes that two things make a religion sacred: the belief in supernatural powers, and the attempt to propitiate or please them.[13] Neale suggests that sacred stories often turn into superhuman entities, or into relics. In turn, they force the faithful to revive them, tremble in their presence, and supplicate them with humility.[14]

I was asked once what I felt when I first beheld the sacred Wailing Wall in Jerusalem. After the Six-Days-War ended in the Middle East, I toured the liberated sections of Jerusalem including the wall. Many casualties were suffered in the freeing of the city, and the wall has become its sacred symbol. It is the only surviving remnant of the Jewish biblical temple, destroyed by Roman soldiers in 70 A.D.

And I recall, upon my arrival, laying eyes on the wall for the first time, the deep disappointment that I felt. I beheld a skimpy wall, which many young boys were killed for. I remember standing there with horror, the question resounding in my head over and over: Is that what we have died for?

Symbols taken seriously and made sacred have enormous power. The strategic and political importance of reuniting Jerusalem, the capital of Israel, has a far greater value than the religious aspect. It is not as dramatic however. Many more people would gladly die in the name of heritage and sacred symbols than for politics or for a strategic position. That too is a ritual.

There are two main scholarly theories regarding rituals. According to one, ritual and myth together constitute the foundation of a culture. They grant people the opportunity to share unique mythologies and special meanings, which create a sense of identification and inclusion. The need for identification and inclusion is very deep in our culture.

According to the second theory, myths serve as social anxiety pacifiers, and rituals support their preservation. In our culture, a prevalent anxiety stems from people's wishes to go on living forever. The myths around a life in the hereafter, and the hope that technology could remedy the organism's mortality, ease this anxiety.

The growing consensus among scholars is that myths rely on rituals for their endurance.

Psychologist T. J. Scheff sheds another interesting light on the subject. He points out that mass entertainment actually competes with religion. Religions produce a collective catharsis and a sense of community similar to that created by films, television, and sports.[15]

The Line between Belief and Make-Believe

> *A majority of people live in between the two poles of disbelief and belief, shuffling back and forth between disappointment and hope. Disbelief may control in most situations, but belief gains ascendancy in times of crisis. The conflict between believing and disbelieving is transcended by make-believing.*
>
> —Robert E. Neale, *In Praise of Play*

Dr. Neale believes that a large part of the response to the supernatural is one of make-believe. For reasons surpassing explanation, many people do not associate believing in the supernatural with make-believe.

I personally know a number of people who innocently make believe that they see, hear, and speak with "spiritual entities," aliens, even deities. However, very few are actually convinced, when pressed. They want to assume it is possible, because it affords comfort and peace of mind. I know from personal experience that a part of them recognizes the fact that they make believe. When we undergo a crisis, for instance, we cry in one manner or another: "Lord, I believe; I want to believe. O help me believe!" This process can be found in many spiritual and self-help books.

Sometimes people go beyond make-believe, as Lisa Beyer illustrates in her article "Crazy? Hey, You Never Know":

> Every year some fifty religious tourists get caught up in the Messianic fever in Jerusalem, and become convinced they are the Savior or another Biblical figure. All are Westerners, about half from the United States and the rest from Western Europe. Christians and Jews share in this equally. On the door of the reception office of a Jerusalem psychiatric hospital, Kfar Shaul, was posted a bumpersticker popular among Orthodox Jews, which reads, "Prepare for the coming of the Messiah." A number of inmates usually claim that they are the Messiah. Sometimes there are two or three Messiahs on premises. They don't fight about it, because, according to a hospital psychiatrist, each is certain that he or she is the one, and that the others are frauds.
>
> One day, an elderly Greek tourist was brought to the hospital in a hysterical condition. She was released when she was diagnosed as free of the danger of assuming divinity. The local Israeli neighbors were concerned simply because they didn't understand Greek, and couldn't know that she was distraught because she got on the wrong bus.[16]

Nothing here is said in a derogatory way, nor contradicts religion. Our relationships with a bank, with an employer, or with the government are religious in nature. They are based on faith and make-believe. Our relationship with religion is basically a spiritual IOU.

At the Rutgers Graduate School of Business Administration we were taught that as corporate executives we should always cover our backs. It's the American way. We called it "the blanket formula." Religion does the same thing; it's an insurance policy against meaninglessness anxiety.

Jessica is a very knowledgeable gardener and a conscientious young worker. Occasionally we call on her to help in our garden.

She is also a devoutly religious person. During one of our conversations, I pointed out to her the freedom we all exercise in manipulating our beliefs. Jessica replied:

"What if what I believe is true? I can't lose."

"No, I suppose not," I responded.

But do we have to take it so seriously? If we didn't take religion and ourselves as solemnly, there would be no inquisition, no persecutions, no genocide, and no crusades. At the same time, we would still be free to enjoy the fantasies and make-believes that religions provide so abundantly.

I conclude this chapter with Neale's account on the rain ritual of the Papagos. The Papagos are American Indians who live in southern Arizona and in the adjacent North Sonora Desert in Mexico. Once a year they participate in a prolonged rain ritual and members of the village prepare a sacred liquid from cactus buds. When the ceremonies begin, the entire village sings and dances and sips from the vat of brewing liquor for two nights. On the third morning, the people gather and sit on the ground in front of the Council Building. A small fire burns at the center. The clergy or medicine man swirls his rattles four times to mark the official opening of the main rite, and begins repeating over and over the rain song:

"At the edge of the mountain a cloud hangs.

And there my heart, my heart, my heart, hangs with it."

Then the men get up and join hands in a clockwise circle
around the fire. All day they dance to the song of the medicine man:

"At the edge of the mountain the cloud trembles.

At the edge of the mountain the cloud trembles."

In the evening, the women get up and join the circle. All night the entire community dances. On the fourth morning the clergy announces:

"Go home now. Sleep. Tomorrow we shall dance again,
that the corn may grow, the beans may grow, the squash may grow."[17]

3

Persona and Performance

We are onlookers as well as actors in the great drama of existence.
—Niels Bohr, *Atomic Theory and the Description of Nature*

A term that may convey the spirit of play more than any other is adventure.
—Robert E. Neale, *In Praise of Play*

Sometimes we live in disharmony because we cannot do the things we think we want to do, only to find out later that they didn't matter, or that we don't really want to do them after all. Likewise, we may be unhappy because the role we are playing does not conform with our, or others', expectations. Actually, what we are looking for is to express ourselves in a way that makes sense to us. My friend Joan once said to me:

"I'm leaving George, because I need space to preserve my sanity."

She was trying to make sense of her existence. After sixteen years of marriage, George's presence didn't really, suddenly, cause her to become insane. Nor did she actually believe that. All she felt was that a change of roles might create a new purpose and a new sense of meaning for her. She was looking for a way to renew her own appreciation of herself.

Behaving and expressing ourselves consciously in roles that authentically corroborate our natures create the feeling that they carry some inherent meaning. Nothing seems to make sense in life when we are confused about the roles we find ourselves playing.

A modification in Joan's roles could accomplish the results she intuitively sought, without having to divorce George and in the process disrupt the economic security and emotional stability of their entire family. Sometimes we can create new roles, activities, and goals for ourselves, in the same way that authors rewrite poorly written novels while using the same pen and keyboard. Artists repaint the canvasses they don't like with their old brushes and chemicals. It isn't necessary to always change partners and scenes, or to resort to some dramatic make-over, to express ourselves in a new way that makes sense to us.

In *Healing into Life and Death,* Stephen Levine relates an anecdote about Loretta, a woman who was dying of cancer. Loretta confided to him during therapy, just as her death approached, that she saw *at last,* only as she was dying, the value of getting on with life. She had been so busy fighting to win over her illness that she hadn't paid attention to the places in herself that had perpetually been distressed, unhappy, and perhaps forever ill. Levine believes that the advent of death acted as a mirror in which Loretta saw—"really saw"—how precious her life was: "It was then that her body began to heal; perhaps life felt safe to her for the very first time."[1]

What I learned from Levine's report is that our preoccupation with wining, in all aspects of life, robs us of the opportunity to feel safe, and condemns us to a life of perpetual struggle with no place to rest. There is a perfectly normal and understandable place to feel helpless or in despair when we are burdened with an illness, pain, and even grief. Existence, then, does not seem to offer the promise of being creative, funny, or joyous. However, a look at ourselves from a perspective of a conscious player of roles interacting with other players of roles can make us realize many things about ourselves, and point out the changes we should make before we act hastily and emotionally without producing a substantial improvement in the end.

This perspective offers a creative way to restructure our inner worlds, by playing with the roles we consciously enact in the external games of society.

Our sad misfortune is, as Americans, that we pride ourselves on being individualists. It has created loneliness that is hard on all of us, especially on persons afflicted with illnesses and fears. Americans, more than citizens of any other industrial nation, fail to understand the meaning of *camaraderie, sharing,* and *support.* Though we use such words quite frequently in our daily rhetoric, we fail to live them.

Our sense of communal intimacy and safety was lost back in the late nineteenth century, with the shift from small businesses to large corporations. This process led to the abandonment, and finally destruction, of our family units. By the 1960s, we gave up completely any veneration, loyalty, and deference that we had toward our elders, parents, and spouses. We lost the traditional and true meaning of family.

With it, we lost the groundedness, security, dependence, love, sympathy, and the sense of belonging and unity that family and small communities awarded their members for centuries. We are on our own even within our immediate families, neighborhoods, workplaces, and clubs. For most of us, homes are no longer our castles. The isolation, fear, confusion, and pain are often unbearable. Direct results of that process are depression and suicide among teenagers, a new and alarming characteristic of our generation.

We may be able to enhance our individual security, personal self-esteem, and emotional well-being by finding a way to restore the traditional family structure with a clear, although revised, designation of duties and responsibilities, and its traditional system of mutual respect and honor. They served us so well for so long, when we were young and old, when we were successful, when we were sick and broke, and when we were happy and unhappy—because we were never lonely or scared. Because we were never as we are now, alone in a harsh and competitive capitalistic world.

A society is formed wherever two or more people dwell. It is the structure we create by defining individual roles designated to each person. Then we move from activity to activity, and from situation to situation, in the same way that a child moves from one game to the next. We love life because, in spite of our afflictions, it can be an adventure. Approaching our environment as a game can make the difference between a life that is mere survival and a life that is enjoyable.

You may have realized by now that my work addresses attitude. I know a woman in Crescent City, California, who is currently writing a book about her Alzheimer-afflicted husband. The book is not a whiner about the miseries of living with an Alzheimer patient, but about the fun-generating episodes and events that she has experienced throughout his long illness. Humor shines even through adversities, even when we are downhearted and in pain; it exists even in the midst of most tragic situations. The comedienne Joan Rivers once said that no misery exists that isn't also potentially very funny.

What I am writing about has nothing to do with making silly jokes or making fun of things. A situation doesn't have to be silly to be joyous. What I am writing about is our attitude.

Most psychologists and physicians emphasize attitude as the central element of healing. Yet few remember that our fears, hopes, struggles, and disappointments, and the actions we take to manipulate them, can be playful and even humorous.

The Meaning of Life for War Prisoners

> *It was obvious that the interests of the people in the camp were really very much like those of people everywhere: their health, where and how they lived, the weather, their work, their neighbors, the inconveniences of life, and of course sex.*
>
> —Langdon Gilkey, *Shantung Compound*

The American theologian Langdon Gilkey taught philosophy at Yenching University in Peking when World War II broke out in the Pacific. The Japanese sent some two thousand Americans and Europeans to a war camp in China, for two and a half years. During his imprisonment, Professor Gilkey recorded his experiences and thoughts. When the war ended, he returned to the United States and taught theology at the University of Chicago. The following is an excerpt from his diary:

> How quickly man makes his life—whatever its character may be—into what he can call "normal." What would have seemed a fantastic deprivation to a man who is comfortable, well fed, and serene in an easy chair at home, had by the end of a few short months become just "life" for us.[2]

The inmates quickly accepted encampment and the fences that kept them inside as their normal life. They were crowded into small spaces, shut off from the outside world, but they griped because their food lines and attendance queues were long and slow. They began to react emotionally only to the new inconveniences of their colony's routine.

Likewise in Europe, Jews in Nazi-occupied regions were required to wear a yellow star to distinguish them from the non-Jewish population. Jewish families throughout the continent were cutting bits of yellow cloth as part of their normal life.

Elie Wiesel is the recipient of a Nobel Prize, as well as of the American presidential and congressional awards and the French Medal of Honor. Strange as it may seem, he wore his yellow star with newfound pride. In *Memoirs*, his autobiography, he writes: "A wretched market sprang up; there were stars of every possible style. Those worn by the rich were bright, those of the poor faded."[3]

Gilkey believes that the human tendency to "normalize" whatever comes is a fortunate trait. He observed that it enabled the war camp inmates to forget their former conveniences, and to accept with equanimity what would have horrified them just a few short months before. The same happened with the Jews in Europe's ghettos and concentration camps, and is true for the elderly, chronically ill, and regular prisoners.

This normalization is possible because of a certain *pretense* we all make: that a new life, one that we learn to bear, is bound to continue without interruption. There is always an expectation—make-believe—that things, as bad as they may be, will not get worse:

> Only thus can mankind live with any serenity amid so much social misery.... Only thus can a person stand the stark insecurity that the next moment may bring to any vulnerable creature![4]

And so, Gilkey tells us, personal relations developed. He met Alice, the British young woman with whom he spent some of his best hours in confinement: "Her good company did more than I can say to make camp life not only bearable, but often gay and pleasant."

It isn't our actual experiences, but what we make of them, which gives meaning to our existence. By defining our roles in a way that makes sense to us in the moment, we forget how flimsy the meaning of existence is.

Robert Landy's Role Categories in Everyday Life

We spend our lives, day-in and day-out,
Thinking, feeling, wondering, what's it all about.
We allude to and seek-out love, ever elusive; it fades away
Like the fleeting colors of a rainbow
Only to return another day.

—Ron J. Flemming, "Colors of a Rainbow"

Psychology professor Robert J. Landy recently wrote an excellent book, as well as an entertaining one, *Persona and Performance*. He classified in it the roles we play in everyday life into five broad categories:

1. Somatic Roles

Roles that are genetically based or inherited, and are necessary to our survival, he calls "somatic": the breather, eater, expeller, sleeper, interactor, and procreator. We don't usually think of them as roles, yet they are. Gender, appearance, health, and age roles are also somatic.

Examples of "appearance roles" are the beautiful, the average, and the beastly. "Health roles" range from the fit to the disabled, and include various dysfunctional roles in-between such as the psychosomatic and hypochondriac. And "age roles" are those of a child, adolescent, adult, and elder. Each somatic role embodies different emotional, intellectual, behavioral, and social qualities. And each has its symbolic characterization in our society.

2. Cognitive Roles

Cognitive roles include the intellectual, the self-deprecating intellectual, the ambivalent, the sage, the critic, the pedant, and the fool. They define our ways of thinking, coping, and solving problems.

Landy uses Shakespeare's Hamlet as a representative individual who assumes a variety of cognitive roles within a short span of time. In Hamlet's case, they were even contradictory roles. He is both simpleton and wise, both able and unable to apply his knowledge toward resolving his existential dilemma, both analytical and irrational, and although he is very intelligent, he is mired in doubt, indecision, and rationalizations.

In real life, Landy writes, "we all play the fool at times." And when we play the pedant, we play the role of people who think they know, thinking that they know that they know.

3. Affective and Moral Roles

These roles are characterized by either moral values or by emotional tendencies: the impulsive extrovert, the compulsive introvert, the virgin, the whore, the martyr, the opportunist, the helper, and the deceiver. They make up the interplay between good and evil, the marks of our social paradigm.

According to Landy, we choose, whether consciously or unconsciously, to undertake the roles of victims and martyrs, or the roles of helpers, healers, and teachers, or the roles of aggressors, angry persons, control freaks, the passionates, or those who deny feelings at all costs. And usually, he says, we play the same roles consistently throughout our lives. In extreme circumstances such as war, a meek person with great inner resources can also perform a single act of heroism.

4. Cultural, Economic, and Political Roles

Cultural roles stem from, and vary with, the political environment. They include the political activist, lobbyist, social rebel, hippie, and today also the feminist and gay. Alongside leadership, authority, and power positions, they are considered cultural "political roles." Businesspeople, corporate executives, lawyers, doctors, farmers, tailors, bartenders, priests, the rich, and the poor, constitute cultural "economic roles."

"Family roles"—daughters, sons, siblings, spouses, parents, and "outcasts" or "pariah roles"—criminals, addicts, and the homeless, are all cultural roles.

5. Spiritual and Aesthetic Roles

A fifth category of everyday roles represents people's religious beliefs, as they are expressed in our society—orthodox, fundamentals, agnostics, atheists, nihilists, or mystics. A subcategory of roles, typically assumed in the arts, consists of painters, dancers, actors, musicians, and authors.

Landy maintains that, for the most part, our primary roles are given to us externally, and that we adopt our secondary roles from our contemporary social circle.[5]

According to Louis A. Zurcher, who teaches sociology and psychology at the University of Texas, the emotions that we display are part of the behavioral script that our society creates for every role. Indeed, we expect parents to display love rather than hatred, social workers to display compassion rather than disgust, and we expect empathy from the clergy.

In his book, *Social Roles*, Zurcher illustrates how our emotions and moods are manipulated and orchestrated in staged events. In weddings and funerals, religious services, sports events, political conventions, talk shows, nightclubs, rock concerts, movies, and graduations, most of us *feel* and behave according to what is expected of us. Those who are not sure what is expected of them usually "look to individuals with whom they are interacting for cues about how to act and to feel."[6]

We are always in role.

Our Analog "I"

I have devoted two years of my life to find my own answers to life's existential questions. Two years is a long time, to be alone with one's thoughts. My first attempts at "aloneness" were far from successful, labeling it "loneliness," everything within me screamed for an alternative. When you are truly alone, you are in the company of only one person, your self. And who was this self, this person? No wonder I felt uncomfortable, I was choosing to spend a great deal of time with someone I didn't know. So my first instinct was to run anywhere, as long as I could avoid this person. The problem, this damned person followed me around like a shadow.

—Louie Rochon, AIDS Awareness Activist

Julian Jaynes taught psychology and consciousness studies at Princeton University. His startling explanation of the nature and evolution of human awareness resonates with all that I have come to understand about the human mind and about the history of the Western mind-set.

In his groundbreaking work, *The Origin of Consciousness in the Breakdown of the Bicameral Mind,* he speaks about the different readouts that our individual "self" displays. He describes personal reality as "buzzing clouds of whys and wherefores, the purposes and reasonings of our narratizations, the many-routed adventures of our analog I's."[7]

One of the distinguishing characteristics of our generation is that so many persons, both young and aging, are "searching" for themselves. At the age of thirty-nine I joined the ranks of the seekers after their "lost self." I even went to India for four months in my search for enlightenment. As innumerable others have done, I called on shrines across the Hindu continent, I stayed in ashrams; I paid tribute to saints and sadhus; and, like many other Westerners, I dwelled in the question made famous by Ramana Maharshi—Who am I?

They say that new sights release the flow of fresh insights. I cannot recall exactly when, perhaps also under a tree, I realized that what I was looking for—my own self—is something I continuously reinvent. I'm always creating fantasy out of actuality, and actuality out of fantasy. The resulting hodgepodge is what I am.

Ever since my enlightenment, whenever I want to know who I am, I look at the role that I enact at the moment. The social roles I fulfill formulate my identity and my self-esteem. As the German-American philosopher Hannah Arendt wrote in her well-known book, *The Life of the Mind:* "Our common conviction that what is inside ourselves, our inner life, is more relevant to what we are than what appears on the outside, is an *illusion.*"[8]

Our reality is made up of concepts. Theories instruct our behaviors and beliefs, and shape our life-styles. Comfort, honor, respect, love, peace, power, and psychological survival are constructs that drive us, and design our daily lives. They become part of our psyche—our motive force, the soul of our actions, the underlying spirit in the roles we play.

A witty cartoon by Cathy, the syndicated cartoon, portrays a middle-aged man, with a full round face and short-trimmed mustache, collecting his personal belongings in a shoebox and walking out of his office:

"You're quitting?" Cathy asks as he walks by her door.

"Everyone's starting to rethink priorities, Cathy," he explains. "We've given all we had to our careers... sacrificed evenings, weekends, relationships, health.... I mean, after fifteen years of killing yourself for a job, you have to stop and ask yourself some pretty major questions!"

"Where's all the money??" Cathy resounds, standing at the door of her office.

An American social psychologist, A. Paul Hare, has pointed out how many of the ideas we have about our real selves are *institutional*. Our feelings, attitudes, and actions originate in economic, political, or religious institutions. We accept and recognize ourselves when we receive validation from others, especially from social or political figures with high visibility.

And, as an American educator William James suggested in 1893, we have as many, and different, selves as there are groups and people whose opinion we value. We show a different aspect of ourselves to our children, to members of our social clubs, to our customers, to our subordinates or supervisors, and to our intimate friends. It is, as Dr. James said, as if we are careful not to let one set of our acquaintances know us as we are elsewhere.[9] Although we look sort of the same person to everyone, it is merely an optical illusion.

We all know that. What we tend to overlook, however, is that not only do we behave and react differently, but we actually think differently in our different roles.

A contemporary philosopher, Nicholas Rescher of the University of Pittsburgh, likewise describes the self—the particular individual that I am—as a mega-process, a system of processes.[10] Indeed, the analog "I" represents various processes of ideas, of feelings, and of desires, and sometimes they contradict each other. I am, and you are, a basket of personas. We merely conceptualize our baskets of Is as if they constitute a single and cohesive entity.

Having acted so many and diverse characters in our lives, each being its own adventure, explains in my view the difficulty that my friend Louie and I have had, and many others too, in knowing coherently who we are.

And one last point. When Jo-Anne was a teenager, she was an alcoholic and a drug addict. At twenty, she was a single mother of two. Jo-Anne was the black sheep of her middle-class family and a burden. Today, fifteen years later, she is married and a respectable middle-aged working woman. A strict mother, she and her two teenage daughters are drug and alcohol free. They are the average American family. But her former drug and alcohol episodes are still part of who she is even in the eyes of those who didn't know her then.

Jo-Anne's name rarely comes up in the presence of new people without mentioning her earlier narrative. This only confirms the fact that all of our actions and activities mirror our multifaceted identities. We are an anthology of diversified and unrelated stories, a collection of all of the roles we have fulfilled and of all of the games we have played.

You and I are an intricate assembly of personas, packaged sound bites and rehearsed lines, arbitrary concepts and unrelated legends bound together in a single volume and under one title.

4

The Theatres of Society

All that we do, all that we think, is just a game, moving shadows; even the creator takes sides.

—Vyasa, *Mahabharata*

"Life is a successful piece of theater,"[1] advanced Eric Bentley, a renowned American playwright. Likened to an immense amphitheater, a society is made up of multiple arenas with their typical scripts and clusters of roles. Wall Street and its stock markets constitute a theatre. Political circles in Washington, DC, are a different theatre. Benedictine monasteries make another stage. And the literary circle of writers in Greenwich Village is quite another. Sociologists call them "reference groups." I refer to them as "theatres."

They exist and operate shoulder-to-shoulder like booths in an immense flea market. They can share space and time, and their actors can have some sort of an exchange. Yet each of us belongs to, lives in, and functions in a particular theatre, participating in its unique drama or game.

Conceptualizing society as one of differentiated theatres has utility in dealing with behavioral expectations of individuals, their compatibility, and challenges. People perceive and define themselves in terms of their roles and arenas. Our titles, uniforms, habits, and modes of communication exhibit it. The stock market and the money game, the corporate business culture, and the literary world of coffee shop poets in Greenwich Village serve as illustrative anecdotes. When we *enroll*, we *enter* a specific *role:* we wear distinct costumes, use special dialects, tune in to particular types of information, and follow selected fads.

In the film *Casino* with Robert DeNiro the Nevada cowboys continue to play by their own rules, which are different from the rules of the game played by the Mafia casino owners: "You all act like you are at home here, but you are not. You are only visitors," says the county commissioner to the Mafia representative (DeNiro). At the end, the Mafia lost their casino and had to leave Nevada.

Except for compulsive consumerism perhaps, we don't have a national cohesive culture that unifies all 270 million Americans. In every little town of about 5,000 inhabitants and upwards various cultures exist simultaneously, groups of people who don't understand each other's mind-set and conduct, who mutually perceive each other as strange or utterly irrational. In the way that we perceive one another, we might as well be aliens from different planets.

Although we commingle in courthouses, in political circles, in colleges, and in workplaces, we dwell and function in our different inner worlds. Sometimes we are suspicious of one another. Sometimes we patronize each other. At times we act against one another. But much of the time we do what we do in spite of one another. The unique culture of each theatre constitutes our attitudes, beliefs, and aspirations, and largely dictates how each of us feels and acts.

Sociologist Peter L. Berger describes it thus:

> Human groups differ in their meaning systems, in the beliefs and perceptions of the world through which they give order and consistency to their actions.... A highly comprehensive meaning system will seek to include all other available meaning systems within itself, interpreting them in its own terms. A less comprehensive meaning system will simply exclude, reject or even fail to perceive other

meaning systems.... Social affiliation or disaffiliation involves specific ways of looking at the world and of conceiving it intellectually.[2]

Consequently, life in any theatre appears different to "insiders" than to "outsiders." To insiders, the game rules make sense and they abide by them, whereas outsiders are not part of that agreement. What transpires inside often seems to be inconsequential to players in other theatres. Yet, conscious participation in society requires us to recognize that such a multitude of games coexist, even within our immediate environment. We cannot objectively evaluate or judge another person, or another game, from the perspective of our own game and rules.

Another film that provides a vivid illustration of the mental affinity that exists between insiders, and that is absent with outsiders—sometimes even when an outsider is close to an insider—is *Subterfuge*. It portrays Peter Langley as a bright, seasoned, and successful British secret service agent after the end of the cold war. Langley becomes a double agent and begins to also spy on England for the Russians. His attractive wife, portrayed by Joan Collins, dislikes spies and stays on the outside. She would rather be married to a publishing vice president with a less lucrative nine-to-five job.

His boss, who suspects that Langley has sold out to the Russians, asks the Americans to send their own agent to spy on Peter Langley. They send Michael Donovan as an attaché to the American Embassy in London. The middle-aged head of the British secret service spends his evenings in an elegant nightclub, sitting at a regular table close to the stage drawing the nude female dancers; this helps him unravel the threats to Britain's national security. Meanwhile, the English double agent surmises that he is under suspicion, and decides to leave his wife and defect to Russia.

All of the participants in this spy drama sympathize with one another. They are motivated by similar forces, and they understand the rules. Except for Langley's wife, who has remained an outsider to the game throughout the years of her marriage, and now despises spies even more.

It is possible to switch fields of activities or games. Modern society is more open and mobile than ever before. But a change from one theatre to another entails a complete transformation from one set of game rules to another. It means a major shift in culture, mind-set, life-style, and language. Dr. Berger described it eloquently, thus:

> The great swindler is a very different figure from the rebel or from the one who withdraws from society. He understands it, operates fully within it, and has all the skills needed to do so successfully. It is not only his morals which separate the swindler from the average citizen, but his perspective on social structure. . . . he sees through the pretense, the "as-if-ness" of society."[3]

Rules of Games

When a person plays, he or she must intermingle with the laws of things and with people in a similarly uninvolved and light fashion. He or she must feel entertained and free of any fear or hope of serious consequences.

—Erik H. Erikson, *Childhood and Society*

This chapter explains game rules and the importance of knowing them. Accurate assessment of the rules, and matching them with individual temperaments, talents, and aspirations, are imperative to our happiness and to life's sense of joy.

In her autobiographical book *bird by bird,* Anne Lamott describes how her public-school lunches were subject to a set of strict rules. She writes:

> It only looked like a bunch of kids eating lunch. It was really about opening our insides in front of everyone. The contents of your lunch said whether or not you and your family were Okay. Some bag lunches, like some people, were Okay, and some weren't. There was a code, a right and acceptable way. It was that simple.
>
> It almost goes without saying that store-bought white bread was the only acceptable bread. There were no exceptions. And there were only a few things that your parents could put in between the two pieces of bread. Bologna was fine, salami and unaggressive cheese were fine, peanut butter and jelly were fine if your parents understood the jelly/jam issue. . ."[4]

Although rules are arbitrary, it doesn't mean that we can avoid them. They give textural consistency to a group. They create a shared set of symbols that make clear to every member what is expected of them, and makes them insiders. Therefore, we cannot ignore prevalent rules and expect to be successful in that particular culture. As newcomers, we cannot substitute them with our own, just because we like our's better. The other participants won't be able to relate to us. Contrary to a popular notion, rules do not limit our freedom; they maximize our freedom, provided we know them and play within their boundaries. That's what makes guidelines so powerful.

One cannot safely assume that the rules of one game will be the same in another. One cannot afford to gamble about their nature either. If abortion is not acceptable in a certain theatre, the players know they have to avoid pregnancies. In monasteries, celibacy is one of the rules, and actors know not to engage in sex. If divorce is a prevalent rule in a particular game, don't be surprised if most participants are divorced or between divorces. Before we enroll, it is helpful if we know the rules of the new game.

Unaware of this law, some people who change games insist on operating by their previous rules. This makes the new game hard and stressful, frequently resulting in a lack of success and no joy. Blame and finger-pointing, which are common at that point, are not the most productive solution: "When in Rome, act as the Romans do," the old saying goes.

The rules of each game cover pretty much all aspects of life, leaving a limited span for individual ideology or personal maneuvers. That is why psychology refers to these rules as "frames." They frame and regulate what is acceptable and what is not acceptable in each game, from life-style and dress code, to conduct, code of ethics, and worldview. They also determine how time is structured, the types of activities that dominate one's life, and the standards for success and personal fulfillment. If playing tennis, golf, or hunting is the norm, you will probably find yourself doing it too. If part of the cultural script is spending evenings in a bar watching sports and drinking beer, you better enjoy doing it with the others or you will be an outsider. If you don't enjoy doing these things, obviously you don't have any business playing their game.

In days of old, royalty and aristocrats, farmers and servants, even slaves, played by rules inherited through tradition and birthright. None of them had the freedom to change or circumvent the rules, to behave or act otherwise than they actually did. An aristocrat could not choose to be a peasant or to behave like a servant, whether they wanted it or not. Social structure would not permit it. An aristocrat had to be a landowner, politician, soldier, or priest. They could not become industrialists, bankers, traders, merchants, or bartenders, the new games that emerged in the seventeenth century and that gave rise to the middle classes of Europe. Indeed, whether in the rigid society that Europe used to be, or in our open culture today, the rules of a given game are still very exacting.

Play Smart—Choose the Right Theatre

The game of professional investment is intolerably boring and overexacting to anyone who is entirely exempt from the gambling instinct; whilst he who has it must pay to this propensity the appropriate toll.

—John Maynard Keynes,
The General Theory of Employment, Interest, and Money

Game? Game? Why did the Master say Game? He could have said business or profession or occupation or what have you. . . . Eighty percent of investors are not really out to make money.

—"Adam Smith," *The Money Game*

When one participates in the wrong game, one sooner or later begins to walk around with the sense that "something" is lacking in one's life, that one is no longer a full partner in the Big Adventure. As someone once admitted at a writers conference: "I can't write my stories to read as interesting as they are when I think them. Perhaps I don't have what it takes to be a writer."

When a particular theatre does not work out, one is free, theoretically at least, to join another. You and I can choose almost any game we wish to participate in, and the role we wish to play in it. By watching others play, we can learn the rules, strategies, skills, and the personal ingenuity that are required in order to function effectively in any particular landscape.

But that isn't enough. Once we grasp the nature of the game, we better make sure that it is also compatible with our individual temperament and talents. To ensure a smooth adjustment, and to be able to perform well, and *enjoy it,* we better make certain that the rules of our chosen game are harmonious with our character as well as with our aspirations.

From my extensive research and experience I have gathered that for a human life to be both fulfilling and "fun," three elements must prevail:

1. a comprehensive familiarity with the rules of one's chosen game;
2. the ability to imbibe and play by these rules comfortably and effortlessly;
3. an ongoing opportunity to express and improve our skill and talents.

In *The Money Game,* "Adam Smith" describes gambling as the game that saves the stock market from being a bore: "I have known a lot of investors," he tells us, who came to the market to make money and succeeded. "So they sat on the dock of their Caribbean home, chatting with their art dealers and gazing fondly at the new sloop, and after a while it was a bit flat, something was missing. . . . The lads with the Caribbean houses and the new sloops have gone back to the game. And they don't have a great deal of time for their toys, the Game is more fun. The real object of the Game is not money, it is the playing of the Game itself."[5]

Choosing the appropriate game is important for making ourselves happy, satisfied, and fulfilled—be it a profession, an activity, or a way of life. A "simple life-style" is a popular concept these days. But if it doesn't suit your temperament, to live "simply" may prove to be stressful and unproductive, not peaceful. I have a friend who became an attorney only to please his parents, because his older brother became a doctor. He would rather be a television host, and he doesn't care about justice. He makes a good living, but his personal life is in shambles.

During the 1980s, I was an international sales manager for a multinational corporation that produces computerized military systems. I came on board after they sold a ten-million-dollar system to a Latin American navy, whose government soon afterward declared a moratorium on all of its foreign payments. To succeed in my new endeavor, I had to be endowed with a fitting personality and a flexible worldview, as the following story illustrates:

The company's only option was to negotiate a barter in lieu of cash payments. A tactic was necessary that would circumvent the law in that country that prohibited barters on military purchases. This entailed the passing of a special act of legislature in their House of Representatives. Being able to pull it off, we would get textiles, fish meal, and miscellaneous second-rate consumer goods. We needed to find a trading organization that would be able to convert large quantities of these commodities into dollars.

Our agent in that country was a retired admiral—short, dark-complexioned, energetic, and well-connected. He knew personally many navy admirals, elected representatives, and government officials. He introduced me to J. Esperito, their powerful mayor. Unlike American mayors, he administered his city from inside jail, after being convicted for accepting bribes. His influence, however, had not diminished and was extremely instrumental to our cause. Initially, the idea of meeting someone within the walls of a prison, however potent, seemed to be appalling. But my concern for the future of the project, and the growing nervousness on the part of our corporate management, persuaded me. I knew that if the deal went through, I could find ideologies that would pacify my conscience.

I went to the meeting in a black limousine, sent for me by the imprisoned mayor. I was let through a few iron gates without much ado by somber guards who didn't blink an eyelash. Matter of routine. The mayor's mother and brother had assured me in an earlier meeting that Esperito would be receptive to our cause and willing to help. Esperito insisted on ritual and ceremonies because he loved the game. I mapped out for him my plan for the barter and the role he was to play. I forgot I was inside a prison until it was time to leave. Making Spanish aristocratic gestures, he rose to shake my hand and accompanied me for a while on my way out.

A few short months later, we were permitted to conclude the barter. We managed to earn over $500,000 after depositing the commissions of various players in Swiss bank accounts. Economic barters, where no money actually changes hands between buyer and seller, enabled foreign corporations like our's to recover losses, and saved a few Latin American governments. Ironically, a decade later barters destroyed the Russian economy after being misused to the point of replacing the domestic cash system.

The test of compatibility is whether we are able to detect, observe, and understand the game ordinances with relative effortlessness. Without such attunement, we may not readily and fully grasp the precepts. We cannot play any game well if we do not seize and wholly embrace its procedures. We must find the rules agreeable and take pleasure in playing by them. Our intrinsic tendencies must be aligned with whatever is necessary for an effective and constructive participation—free of psychological, physical, or emotional friction. Or the game becomes a strain to endure, and the player fails or burns out.

I have known individuals who bounce around from game to game, from one field to another, without ever figuring out the game or role most suitable for them. It requires work to learn a game, and it takes courage to assess one's own nature. Knowing ourselves, our true strengths and weaknesses, is not only relevant but consequential to making the right choices. Concurrently, a definitive familiarity with the rules and structure of a game and its environment often bring into view opportunities that match our personality traits, and that become available to us. Under certain circumstances such a match may affect or change one's destiny.

Twenty Political and Two Business Roles

In his engaging book, *Shantung Compound*, Professor Langdon Gilkey offers an interesting observation about the roles that politicians and business people play in society. He describes the power games that went on in his war camp in China during World War II. His own natural qualities as an educator come through his writing:

> During our stay there, this problem of politics, of our own self-government and self-direction, remained to me the most subtle, the most frustrating and baffling issue we had to face. It was also the most fascinating, as I discovered very early.
>
> There was no camp chairman, no government, not even a chairman of the meeting; all such posts of authority were still "up for grabs."... Whatever dominance a man achieved in that group, he gained through inherent personal capacity for power.[6]

A capacity for power, he went on to suggest, is composed of some basic intangible qualities that cause authority to gravitate to, and then remain with, a particular individual. Among these qualities are an ability to think quickly and relevantly, great self-confidence, iron firmness of will, and boundless personal energy. In the war camp, Gilkey witnessed how someone who has these qualities can in a short time stand alone over the others.

Soon a political struggle developed between twenty members of the camp's self-appointed leadership committee. By the end of the first week, a hierarchy of power already appeared. A few men gained subtle dominance, and the others began to wait to hear what these few would say before they suggested anything themselves: "At this point, only the great dared challenge the great; the rest had given up the fight. They would rather now be secure on the side of the winner than reach for the glory of power only to find themselves defeated, isolated and humiliated. So, without any external force, even without a hint of a ballot, but only by the quiet process of self-elimination, the list of contenders had been reduced to two or three giants who were still able to contend for the role of Caesar."[7]

Just as captivating, is Gilkey's perception of the unique character and value of the businessperson's role, what he calls the "mentality of decision." Two members of the camp committee were businesspeople who before the war participated in a scholarly discussion group in Peking. In that group, Gilkey and other academics used to debate abstract issues, such as peace, international justice, and the relations of ethics or theology to the world of affairs. The academics flowed with verbiage. By contrast, the two businesspeople kept silent, though observant, polite, and respectful: "Nice, responsible men, but hardly bright—surely not able to think," was Gilkey's initial impression of them.

Yet in the camp, suddenly:

> the minds of these men, accustomed to practical problems that called for both know-how and decisiveness, clamped onto our situation and dealt with it creatively. What was needed here were concrete answers to technical and organizational problems. To be facile in the area of abstractions or of general truths was of no help when the oven walls were cracked, when the yeast wouldn't raise the

bread dough, when slightly smelly meat was delivered in hot weather. Now it was the professional mentality that was proving useless, and the academic voices that were strangely silent. I could see the concrete need only after they had pointed it out to the Japanese; I could recognize the neatness of their solution only after they had explained it to us.[8]

As Robert J. Landy also recognized, all of our activities are games in which our psychic struggles get played out.[9] Thus, summarily, an accurate assessment of the rules of the game we choose to play against our individual temperament, natural talents, and aspirations, is imperative for our happiness and for the joy that we can derive from life.

Another benefit is that if we can grasp that society is a composite of parallel theatres, each with its own game, and set of rules and culture, then we may not be so quick and harsh in our judgments of other people's behaviors and attitudes. To understand others requires us to make an effort to understand their actions and lives in the context of their own game, theatre, and the rules that go with it.

5

Think, Don't Believe

Custom does not breed understanding, but takes its place, teaching people to make their way contentedly through the world without knowing what the world is, nor what they think of it.

—George Santayana, *Skepticism and Animal Faith*

Philosophy works slowly. Thoughts lie dormant for ages, and then, almost suddenly as it were, mankind finds that they have embodied themselves in institutions.

—Alfred North Whitehead, *Science and the Modern World*

Thinking, not believing, is the road to enlightenment. Falsehood occurs, said Augustine, when something is believed to be that is not. This world is a comedy to those who think, and a tragedy to those who feel, observed the English historian Horatio Walpole. Since anything that is true can be arrived at through cogitation, rather than through feeling or blind faith, I ask you to ponder it.

I met Melissa in 1974. She was a beauty, curly brown hair, gentle face and body features, and five feet five inches tall. I enjoyed watching her graceful movements. She had blue, wise eyes, and hardly wore makeup or perfume, naturally fresh.

Her father was a Baptist minister in North Carolina. Melissa had just returned from her father's speaking tour in Europe, and came to New York to select a college. That is when I met her.

Beholding her for the first time, I fell in love. I was twenty-six; she was nineteen.

We went out to dinner at an elegant downtown restaurant. It was small and cozy, white tablecloths, glittering candles, live music, and a real fireplace. As we entered, I asked to be seated at a romantically quiet table.

We stared at one another all evening, while I told her about my new position right out of graduate school. Clearly overtaken, she didn't remove her shining eyes from my face for three hours. During that time I devoured a half pound of filet mignon and a baked potato with sour cream, but she hardly touched her's. What seemed to be her deep interest in me caused my mind to whirl in La-La fantasy land. All I could think of was our naked young bodies together after dinner, in bed. I couldn't wait to leave the restaurant. When the waiter came to suggest dessert, she didn't even hear him. I motioned the man to leave us alone.

"The food is very good. If you're not hungry, you can take it to go," I suggested.

"Oh yes, the food is excellent, but really, I'm not a big eater," she replied bashfully. And then, with hesitation, she added: "Can I ask you a personal question? I've been wanting to . . . "

"Of course, Melissa, ask anything." My healthy heart, belonging to a youthful male body with hyper hormones and active imagination, began to race.

"You are Jewish; aren't you?" came the question I was unprepared for.

"Yes. But you knew that. Is that a problem?" I prayed for a no.

"No, no problem." (I sighed with relief, quickly thanking God for answering my prayer.) "I'm curious about something, although I'm ashamed of it," Melissa continued. "You see, you are the first real Jew that I have ever met. Prior to today, I saw only pictures of Jews in books; in them, they always have horns."

"Have you been looking for my horns, Melissa?"

"Yes, I'm sorry." I began to kiss my fantasy good-bye.

"I'll be honest with you," I confided. "I was looking forward to spending the night with you."

"Oh no! I couldn't. Not because you're Jewish. I must save it for my wedding night, with my father being a minister!"

I have often thought of pretty, gentle Melissa over the years. As it turned out, since I don't have horns like Moses, David, and the Elks, we never met again.

Linda had worked as a secretary in my office in southern California for about a year, in 1992. Of medium height and slim, usually wearing Givenchy's Ysatis perfume, Linda was an attractive woman in her late thirties. She was financially independent, twice divorced. One day she said to me:

"Why do you accept so many Jewish and Israeli clients?"

While I was taking my time to come up with an appropriate response to what I considered an inappropriate question, Linda, who had graduated from the University of California, proceeded to explain why she didn't like to work with minorities:

"Minority people are weird. They have accents, and I have difficulty understanding them. It makes my work harder."

"I have an accent," I replied. "Does that make me weird?"

"Not you. But most of them are," she said.

I was aware of the fact that she frequented a progressive new-age church, Science of Mind, on Sundays. So I volunteered:

"Christ must have had an accent. The same accent, as a matter-of-fact. Till his death, he was a traditional Jewish man. That doesn't make him weird, does it?"

It was now Linda's turn to take time to ponder an appropriate response. Finally, her brown eyes gazing at me, she mumbled:

"You know, I've heard this before, of course! But I still cannot *accept* the fact that Christ is a Jew."

Changing one's beliefs is not easy. We hold onto what we consider to be our truths in order to feel safe, to find comfort, or to explain to ourselves something in a way that would resolve internal conflicts.

To survive economically, we play all sorts of games with each other, as we shall see throughout this book. But to survive psychologically, we usually play games with ourselves. We make believe that what we give credence to must be true, and we refuse to accept something else as valid. This does not impact our own view of ourselves as liberal, progressive, and modern thinkers.

Sometimes it is difficult to think clearly through something we strongly believe in, as in Linda's case regarding Christ, or Melissa's understanding of Jews. Had I not met Melissa, I would have had a hard time accepting the idea that there were Americans in the 1970s—whether or not as educated and well-traveled as Melissa—who still believed that Jews have horns.

On 11 May 1986 the *New York Times* reported that in Paris a French diplomat, Bernard Bouriscot, and a Chinese opera singer were sentenced to jail for six years. For twenty years, the diplomat had a love affair with the Chinese actress without knowing that "she" was a man and a professional spy. During that period he continually passed classified information to Mr. Shi, whom he thought to be a "she." Bouriscot testified that in twenty years he never saw Mr. Shi naked. He *believed* that modesty is a Chinese custom.[1]

Such stories repeatedly bring to mind the old dictum that knowledge of life doesn't come through emotional experience, but through intellectual understanding and empirical grasp. The only objective fact is that we are alive. Everything else we know is often more imaginative than reality. It's alright if one *consciously* plays life; otherwise one may feel cheated and a fool when the truth surfaces.

When I shared these thoughts with my physician-friend Shelby, she chuckled:

"Here you go again with the idea that life ought to be treated as a game."

"Well," I said, "we either survive life long-faced, or we experience it *fully*. Living fully often means toying with life, and conscious toying is a game. But whatever we do, we must not take it too seriously."

My friend Louie Rochon is a great walker and a profound thinker. He recently walked over five thousand miles across the United

States, from Florida to Seattle. It provided him with space and time to think, and in the process he raised Americans' awareness toward AIDS among heterosexual children. He shared with me the following excerpt from his diary, which, I believe, applies to many conscious individuals:

> A simple look back into my past convinced me that running and pretending, living in a fantasy of who I would like to be as opposed to who I am, failed to serve me anymore. I also found that exhausting my mind by replaying the same outdated thoughts over and over, like an endless loop tape, rarely allowed me the insights I was seeking. I was stuck. It was time for some new thoughts, a fresh new set of beliefs.

There is constant activity in our lives; things always happen. But it helps if we remember that some things happen to us because we are in each other's faces. And that although we may share the stage, more often than not we are participating in separate games. When our games cross, we may find ourselves acting in a movie that is not about ourselves. I'm not always the real star of my show. Yet, like me, the other players also get caught up in their activity, and believe that the film is about them and that they are the star. Planet Earth has one life and about six billion actors. Each one believes that they have a leading role, that the movie of Earth is about them.

We dwell and function in the environment of our stories and theories. We call them "beliefs," "faith," and "reality." They pretty much dictate the themes of our inner scripts, what Louie described as endless loop tapes. If we can perceive our thoughts and beliefs as scripts, we understand that we don't have to take even them too seriously.

A Game Called "Advertising"

I don't care what is written about me so long as it isn't true.

—Katherine Hepburn

I glanced at the newspaper that lay on my reading table. An advertisement read: "Come to our restaurant . . . the place where your dreams come true." My wife and I go to restaurants to procure reasonably priced tasty but preferably healthy nourishment. But for many people apparently a restaurant can be a place where fantasies come true. That's why advertising professionals can portray people who are perpetually comfortable and blissful, and who get readily ecstatic over a mundane tossed salad.

This, for instance, was an actual TV commercial for a salad dressing: Three couples got together for dinner in someone's home. In the kitchen, they prepare the salad in a frenzy of rapture. They giggle joyously as they slice, dice, and toss the succulent lettuce. When they top the greens with the featured dressing, the six reach a collective high. Rolling their eyes and licking their lips, they moan and laugh hysterically.

For how many people does a salad, any salad, produce such ecstasy? When we buy into our advertising campaigns, it is possible for us to feel inadequate because our immediate experience does not support their idyllic portrayal of, let's say, happy people. But advertising is only a game. By taking the advertising game seriously, we lend ourselves to being deceived and misled. One of the things that this work endeavors to accomplish is to show how many elements in our everyday lives are games that we play with each other, consciously or unconsciously.

In his extraordinary book *Games People Play*, the psychiatrist Eric Berne describes what he calls the "alcoholics' game." As in every other human drama, here too, various personalities play roles, not always consciously.

The Game Alcoholics Play

In the alcoholics' game, the main actor is the alcoholic. In Berne's narrative the alcoholic is a man called "Mr. White." There are three supporting roles: The "Persecutor," usually a spouse. The "Rescuer," often a friend, or a family physician who is interested in drinking problems, possibly a secret alcoholic; at a later stage, the role of Rescuer may be taken over by a sponsor from Alcoholics Anonymous. And the "Patsy," often a mother who keeps giving money to the alcoholic, sympathizing with the alcoholic son's difficulty with a less-than-understanding spouse.

At times, the alcoholic's spouse may play all three supporting roles. She can be the Patsy who makes coffee for her alcoholic husband when he comes home at night drunk. She may even let him beat her up before he passes out on the floor, then drag him into bed, undress, and tuck him in. The next morning she may take on the role of the Persecutor and berate him for his behavior. And later, while serving him dinner, she can become the Rescuer who pleads with him to cease drinking, maybe even threatening him for the thousandth time that she will leave him if he doesn't stop getting drunk.

When Mr. White decides to join Alcoholics Anonymous, the change of scene also brings a change in the supporting actors. Former alcoholics, says Berne, make more effective Rescuers—"because they know how the game goes, and hence are better qualified to play the supporting role." The pleasure of the hangover, he says, not the joys of intoxication, keeps alcoholics in the game and in the gutters. Alcoholics are immune to the physical pain. What they cannot bear is the psychological agony that is behind their drinking.

After awhile, the alcoholic often decides to move forward with his game—he stops drinking. That is a day of great consequence, when the alcoholic and his Rescuer get together to celebrate six dry months without drinking. They congratulate each other on both their efforts and shared success. The next evening, according to Berne, White is often found sprawled in the gutter, and the game starts all over again. When a chapter of Alcoholics Anonymous runs out of active alcoholics to rescue, the Rescuers themselves sometimes resume drinking, to continue to play their game.[2]

Consciously or unconsciously, we are constantly acting out a drama. Our lives are a series of games all the way to the very end. Our serious attitude toward them does not change their nature. Performers on stage also take their acting very seriously, although they know that they are acting a role. This insight can provide a shortcut to healing.

With this type of acknowledgment, alcoholics may be able to play out their psychological drama without reaching the gutter. They may choose another game to play, less destructive, which will bring them a similar emotional payoff. They may even quit the game altogether and move on to live a healthy and productive life, thus getting rid of their tendency toward self-destruction.

By becoming conscious life players, we can step back and observe our act, then find the way to change the game we play. We do not have to continue to be motivated day after day by unconscious emotional processes just because their unraveling requires some mental work and clear thinking.

The Drama of Suffering

> *I have known a time when young people were singing from morn to eve, they were caroling both out-and-in-doors, behind the plows as well as at the thrasher floor and the spinning wheel. This was all over long ago. Nowadays there is silence everywhere; if someone was to try and sing in our days as we did of old, people would term it bawling.*
>
> —Johas Stolt (Swedish peasant)

There's a significant distinction between physical and emotional suffering. In the contemporary use of language, we use the word *pain* to describe everything—from strokes and headaches to disappointment over a relationship breakup, from child abuse to loss of a job or failure to win a marathon.

I prefer to use the word *pain* to describe physical aches, and the word *suffering* for emotional agony. The rationale for it is simple: while physical aches occur in the body, emotional suffering takes place in the mind. In contrast to bodily aches, the suffering around a loss or pain is a mental agony.

As humans, our experience of suffering has grown as we have learned to think and to process mentally. As far as we can observe, most animals undergo pain but not as much suffering. Whatever suffering we witness in our pets and other mammals is due to their ability to think and process concepts, as we do, though in varying degrees.

Scientific evidence suggests that just as we can perceive physiological distress, we can numb it. Schizophrenic patients, for instance, are less sensitive to it. Their bodies create more endorphins in response to stress, which allows them to be oblivious to pain. A lower attention span also diminishes suffering. A direct correlation has been found to exist between our level of mental attention, our tolerance of physical pain, and the psychological agony we create around it. And so I've come to see that much of our mental suffering is drama.

Dr. George Von Bekesy was a Nobel laureate in physiology and medicine at Harvard. In the late 1960s he conducted a series of experiments with blindfolded people. Some of them felt sensations in one knee that actually belonged to the other knee, while others felt aches in the space between their knees. Participants in Von Bekesy's experiments mentally experienced pain even in amputated legs and arms.[3]

Adultery was considered such a terrible offense in the nineteenth century that it caused many men and women to become gravely ill. In our own generation, however, the pain related to adultery is rapidly diminishing since it is no longer perceived as an affront to self-esteem.

Likewise, because we operate in a mode where everything is serious and important, we tend to create undue drama about a lot of things. That causes both our mind and body to tighten up, worries and aches spiral, and we spin in suffering. With the lost peace of mind, we also lose peace of heart. Conversely, as many scientific books suggest, conscious role-play tends to generate enthusiasm and vigor, releasing a vast amount of confined energy that often transforms into pain and emotional strain in inhibited individuals.[4]

Play in Sickness

To individuals who suffer from a physical, mental, or emotional illness, a playful attitude toward life may appear absurd. Particularly when one is afflicted with a fatal or chronic ailment. Under such circumstances, joy and happiness often take a different meaning.

A question that often arises is whether it is necessary for existence to be an uninterrupted pleasure, completely free from excruciating pain, to be considered fun or to be treated as a game. This is just one of the rules of the game of being alive, and my purpose here is not to indulge in hackneyed assertions about pain, the spiritual lessons of illness, or about the inevitability of death. I merely endeavor to shed some light on the difference between physical pain and mental suffering, in order to enable interested readers to relate to life as sport even while it contains aches and sorrows.

Stephen Levine works with individuals who dying or are terminally ill. With his wife Ondrea, he taught meditation in the

California prison system, led healing workshops, and collaborated with Ram Dass and Elizabeth Kubler-Ross. They observed many people who, before dying, healed long-pained minds, thus achieving peace of heart. In his gripping book, *Healing into Life and Death,* he states:

"It became obvious that there wasn't something spiritually or psychologically amiss with those who didn't cure their bodies. . . . The confused elitism that somehow those who heal their body are 'better' than those who don't, has a tendency to come back as a sense of failure on the death bed, when the last disease inevitably comes along and displaces us naturally from the body."[5]

Berne relates the story of a man with a wooden leg. During World War II, the man went around army hospital amputation centers and demonstrated to their patients, very competently, jitterbug dancing, a strenuously acrobatic jazz jig with twirls, splits, and somersaults.[6]

The world does not have to be held responsible for ailments. It is not necessary to hold life guilty, or to punish it by refusing to play.

In 1967 during the Six-Days-War, I was wounded and consequently lost the hearing in my right ear. While chasing the Egyptians, we drove into a mine field. Bodies of my men became scattered on the yellow dry sand of the Sinai desert. I was five feet 6 inches tall, but husky and strong. I was trained to run uphill carrying men on my shoulders who were much bigger and heavier than myself. So I got up and began to evacuate the bodies with the medics. Some of my men were dead; most of them were wounded. At last, I also climbed into the ambulance and lost consciousness, which I regained as we were pulling into a field hospital. I tried to get up, but a faint dizziness kept me glued to the bench of the ambulance. The last one into the ambulance, I was the first to be carried out:

"I'm fine," I said to the two medics who reached for me.

"Your head is cut open; you're bleeding," a faceless medic said to me.

"This blood belongs to my men . . . " I mumbled.

A medic touched my head and examined the fresh red fluid on his hand. I stared at the blood. I felt no pain; I was still in shock. The two medics hauled me away on a stretcher. Within hours, head bandaged, I was flown by helicopter together with other wounded soldiers to an army hospital inside Israel. Two subsequent surgical attempts failed to restore my ability to hear in my right ear.

For years I ignored this handicap. Being suddenly hard of hearing in my early twenties was a terrible affront. I hid my disability from people for thirty years, afraid to disclose it for fear of rejection. Instead, I acquired a habit of slightly bending my head to the right, exposing my healthy left ear to a wider range of sounds. During conversations I automatically turn my left ear slightly toward my speaker and I concentrate. It's subtle. Most people never notice. The good ear has learned to cover for its deaf partner.

In college I always sat in the front row focusing intently on the professors' lips. I cannot describe their eyes or noses, but I remember their mouths. If I mentioned to anyone that I was hard-of-hearing, they would often avoid talking to me afterward. As we know, differences frighten people. We tend to resent and resist almost anything that is unlike ourselves. And yet it is variety that we look for in entertainment, which makes our lives exciting and interesting. A strange predicament.

My sense is that most members of our society don't know how to speak to a deaf or half deaf human being. We don't learn how to play this role unless we live with a hearing-impaired person. And what is unknown and unfamiliar somehow makes us feel awkward, and therefore is threatening to us.

Since most verbal exchanges around me sound as nothing more than incoherent noise, I developed the habit of ignoring general communication between people in my vicinity. Out of this grew a strong tendency not to engage in conversations unless I am addressed directly. And then I often respond with: "What did you say?" I'm never certain whether my listeners hear me clearly. I repeatedly ask if I'm being understood. Occasionally, someone retorts:

"Why do you keep asking that; do you think I'm stupid?"

"No, of course not."

I tend to speak loudly because I need to hear my voice, to distinguish it from inner sounds. Most of my colleagues in business and social circles have attributed my manner of speaking to a Middle Eastern culture. Israelis, like Italians and Greeks, are notorious for enthusiastic articulation. To date, my wife periodically says:

"Dear, I'm right here. You don't have to speak loud now."

I used to wonder how I come across to various listeners—passionate, overpowering, insistent, empathic, angry, enthusiastic, or entertaining? It depends, I learned, on each spectator's individual experience and past encounters. Once, an agitated young man said to me:

"I want to hear what you're saying. But I can't when I'm being shouted at!"

My ears turned purple, yet I didn't offer an explanation.

I used to believe that a person with a handicap, or a disease, cannot treat life lightly. That the attitude of conscious role-play is appropriate only when one is not afflicted with AIDS or cancer, certainly not when one is dying. I insisted that this privilege belongs only to those who always feel good and are perfectly healthy. I've experienced directly how a chronic disability and being subject to constant pain can make it formidable to view life as game.

I also learned that preoccupation with one's misery can fog the possibilities for roles one still can play in society or in one's immediate environment. I discovered that by "playing" life, we get to select and modify roles according to our strengths and limitations.

Nancy Mairs, in an article that offers advice to women authors, cites a woman afflicted with a chronic illness acknowledging that it is possible to be simultaneously sick and happy: "This good news, once discovered," she said, "demands to be shared."[7]

We still regard this as a novel attitude. But many distinguished leaders in the healing professions have been saying these words now for more than a half century. It is possible to have a joyous, playful, and balanced life even when the body continues to be ill and in pain. Treating life playfully brightens gloomy days, lifts downhearted spirits, and energizes tired muscles and minds. It lightens the burdens of existence.

Part 2

Success Redefined

Like a heartfelt handshake
Life is what we make
Guessing all the while;
Trying to do our best
Being honest to ourselves
Working to pass the test
Caring about our health;
A good attitude is the key
To the door that swings open
Allowing us to be free
Putting happiness in motion....

—Ron J. Flemming, "New Year"

6

Can Work Be Playful?

Play is more than a name applied to a given list of activities. It is an attitude which may pervade every activity.

—Luther Halsey Gulick, *A Philosophy of Play*

There are two Western schools of thought about the relationship between work and play: One school makes a deliberate distinction between play and work. The other school maintains that play is an attitude of mind that may pervade any human activity.[1]

The proponents of the latter school believe that insisting on categorizing everything neatly into play and nonplay is misleading, counterproductive, and the cause of much stress. With Johan Huizinga, they feel that labeling playful attitude as "nonserious" turns every playful activity in our minds into an activity that isn't productive or important. Yet we have seen how pervasive role-and-game play are in our culture. In fact, they are the basis for functioning in an organized manner; they are the matrix of civilized society. Somehow, it resonates better with the Western ear when we address, or define, our busy activities as "playful" rather than as "a game."

Social psychologist Susanna Millar offered an elegant solution to our linguistic predicament: to define play as an *attitude,* not as a *type of activity*.[2] Instead of distinguishing between work and play as types of activities, we can talk about a *playful* or *nonplayful* attitude.[3] Dr. David L. Miller explains it most eloquently: "Not that we should stop working and start playing, but we should work as if at play. Because that is what we are doing anyway, playing at work."[4]

Our most advanced training programs utilize role-play and games. Universities, corporations, governments, and military forces play extensively in order to achieve in-depth understanding and enhance decision making, and in order to develop skills and cultivate attitudes. It also serves to brighten and vitalize dreary routine work.

The most renowned person to bring play into business and work was the Jewish mathematician and physicist John Von Neumann. His *Theory of Games of Strategy*, which was published in 1926 and was first adopted by the United States military, mirrored the reality of the workplace.

Games of Strategy

John Von Neumann was a quantum physicist. He immigrated to the United States from Hungary in 1931 and taught at Princeton University. He was one of the developers of the American hydrogen bomb and of cybernetics, and is considered to be the inventor of the digital computer.

Von Neumann was aware of the fact that people do not always behave rationally. Therefore, he decided to utilize conscious game playing to enhance decision making in conflict situations. As a game theorist, he focused on our uncertainties, which originate in our and in other people's unknown intentions. As in games, most important decisions in business and politics are arrived at through a series of negotiations. A negotiation, in turn, is a process during which each side compromises something in order to reduce the risks of uncertainty. Today everyone knows that successful bargaining is a chain of staged acts designed to award either side a greater gain than would be otherwise possible.

Although the game theory was intended for public policy and decision makers, it applies to every one of us in day-to-day situations. It is true for individuals, corporations, organizations, and nations. Many people often find it very hard to make up their minds or to follow a series of activities in a consistent manner. It is hard not to give in to conflicting pressures. Consequently, without well-defined, consistent objectives and game-rules, most people are not expected to behave consistently, rationally, or in a utilitarian manner. Therefore, the game theory is not so much a theory as it is quite an accurate description of social behavior where rationality and consistency are imperative for the productivity of individuals and normal functioning of society.

In 1938, Oskar Morgenstern, a celebrated economist from Vienna, migrated to the United States. He met Von Neumann at Princeton University, and in 1944 they published their classic book *The Theory of Games and Economic Behavior*, tailored for the business community. Its impact on economic theory in recent years has been significant. In addition, it was soon expanded to other social sciences as well.

Social scientists have realized that games do not necessarily render an activity frivolous or inconsequential. Very serious pursuits in the military, industry, domestic politics, and education have benefited from it. In 1982, for instance, Dr. Alan Blinder, also an economist from Princeton University and vice-chairman of the Federal Reserve, applied the game theory to activities relating to the planning of the federal government's budget and monetary policy.

Decisions in Washington, DC, are frequently self-serving and irrational. They are reached every day through a process of resisting political opponents, in which role-players get caught up in private games. You and I, constituting the voting public at large, are not parties to the policy-making process, although we are greatly impacted by it. The competition among interest groups aiming to influence America's domestic and foreign public policies are political games that private groups play in order to outmaneuver or overwhelm opposing groups, seeking to pressure the legislature to protect their economic interests or to place their ideologies on the public agenda. During the 1980s and 1990s, the number of interest groups playing the political game has grown significantly, and subsequently the mix of interests that make up the public agenda has dramatically expanded. Political scientists increasingly explain the incoherence of our public policies as the outcome of the game that interest groups play.[5] Game theory has forced Congress and state politicians to consider not only interest groups but also the needs of the American people.

Lawrence P. Jacks, a Unitarian minister and professor of philosophy at Oxford University, commented on the contribution of game theories to education. According to Jacks, the discovery of the educational promise of play may be counted as one of the greatest realizations of the twentieth century.[6] Many contemporary social scientists support his claim, noting how conscious game and role-playing stirs human intelligence to ever-higher levels, with less effort and greater efficiency than conventional methods.

And in *The Money Game,* a revealing book about our attitudes toward the stock market, "Adam Smith" wrote:

> The [stock] market is both a game and a Game, i.e., both sport, frolic, and play, and a subject for continuously measurable options. If it is a game, then we can relieve ourselves of some of the heavy and possibly crippling emotions that individuals carry into investing. . . . Game Theory has had a tremendous impact on our national life. It influences how our decisions are made, and how the marketing strategies of great corporations are worked out.[7]

The Multimillion-Dollar Executive Games of Virtual Reality

If games were nonsense, what else would there be left to do?

—Leo Tolstoy

A corporation I worked for in the 1980s is producing gigantic virtual reality systems for military use. Global wars across lands and oceans are simulated on monitors, fought, and analyzed. Armies, navies, and air forces are integrated to enable strategic planning and decision making at all levels.

The players are generals, admirals, submarine and aircraft-carrier commanders, and combat pilots. They spend weeks training behind enemy lines—in a virtual environment. They sit in front of powerful graphic monitors that simulate varied military functions including artillery, communication, and headquarters, using aerial views of actual landscapes. They maneuver their forces from one place to another and enact warfare on virtual battle grounds. They fly airplanes, sail ships, drive tanks, and walk within the three-dimensional space of their terminals, navigating their own images, and their vehicles and instruments, by merely employing body and hand gestures.

The computers simulate environmental conditions and influences, including such sensory inputs that fighters encounter in actual cockpits, submarines, and tanks. The officers experience and respond to them. They *feel* as if they are actually flying in the simulated airplanes, sailing or moving on the ground in every direction. When they have to enter buildings, doors open and close and they "walk" through them. The interactive computer system is "so fast and so intuitive that the computer *disappears* from the mind of the user, leaving the computer-generated environment as the reality,"[8] using L. Casey Larijani's narrative in *The Virtual Reality Primer*.

This is play.

According to scientific findings, the longer one stays in virtual reality, the easier it becomes to suspend one's knowledge and beliefs about the external world. One becomes so enmeshed in the game that its environment becomes reality. Someone phrased it eloquently: "Your head believes it, and the rest of you goes along for the ride."

Although they are carried out playfully, these games are work. The future of wars, nations, lives and deaths, and the ability of our high-ranking officers and executives to think in critical situations, very much depend on these games. They are anything but frivolous. As Oscar Morgenstern acknowledged in his foreword to Morton Davis's book *Game Theory*, these games represent the immense complexity of our society.

A major department store in Japan operates virtual reality boutiques. Larijani describes it in his book *The Virtual Reality Primer* as a total sound, sight, smell, and touch system that simulates merchandising departments on monitored stations. Using data-gloves and 3-D glasses, the customers enter a virtual store that exists only on screens, yet gives them the illusion that it is suspended in the space in front of them.

In the housewares department, for instance, shoppers can virtually create an entire kitchen, on the screen, with the aid of appropriate gloves and goggles. Incorporating their own ideas as well as designs provided by the store, they plan the cabinets they fancy, run virtual water, select the appliances they want, and check them as if they are real. Then they can order the equipment, or an entire kitchen, without ever speaking to a living salesperson. Everything, including the contract, is generated in virtual reality.[9]

We are all familiar with the proverb, there is a child hidden in every man and woman, and this child wants to play. We merely move from game to game.

The most recent development in the Western world is the Internet. It brings into our homes a new and rapidly expanding virtuality. The individuals we interact with through e-mail, but never meet, are virtual personalities with whom we engage as if they are real. As more of our social exchange, professional work, household purchasing, and study activities occur on the Internet, the more detached we become from our actions. That is play.

As we evolve, so do our games.

I believe that dreams and meditations are also games, psychological ones. My wife once dreamed that she lost me in a crowd. I was a German shepherd, and we lived in New York where large herds of people routinely flock in the streets. Our building doorman had gone home for the evening, and she was worried that I, being a dog, wouldn't be able to enter our apartment building on my own. At that time we actually lived in a house in the country and our dog was a white-tipped gray Keeshound with a thick white tail. In the mental game of her dream, my wife was married to a cute guide dog, a large black-and-tan bushy-tailed German shepherd.

Whether we dream mind games, or whether we play games in the military, education, industry, social, and networking organizations, they *feel* very real to us and therefore we take them seriously.

Vacationing on the Austrian Alps

Educators and scholars have been protesting that role- and game-play are still considered derogatory concepts in our culture, ever since the Roman Catholic Church prohibited play in the eighteenth century. An incredible survey has revealed that many people are either unaware, or do not believe, that they are free to be playful about serious matters. When they know that it is allowed, they often find it difficult to be playfully serious. However, noted scientists like the psychiatrist Eric Berne point out that a playful spirit changes our posture, voice, viewpoint, and tolerance. As a result, we feel better about ourselves and consequently about the event at hand.[10]

Work is utilitarian and weighty, so pervasively joyless. To escape work, we go to extremes to create entertainment for ourselves instead of making a simpler effort to enjoy our work; for instance, in 1991, I went to a Halloween party in Phoenix, Arizona, thinly dressed in a Julius Caesar outfit. The festivities took place in the open cool air of an enchanting garden. By midnight, most of the guests were a bit tipsy and we jumped stark naked into the swimming pool. I returned home from the trip with pneumonia.

My wife and I and my parents spent a three-week vacation on the Austrian Alps, to celebrate their fiftieth anniversary. We stayed in the picturesque resort town of Seefeld, at a charming bed and breakfast that overlooked the famous mountains that range from Italy to Switzerland.

My seventy-year-old mother laughed all the time. I was amazed. We hadn't seen my parents for two years, and it was inconsistent with my memories of her. While strolling on the promenade, I put my arm around her shoulder and asked:

"Mom, what makes you laugh so much?"

"It's funny, so I laugh," she replied absentmindedly.

"What's funny, Mom?" I insisted.

"Well, we, for example. Don't you think we are funny? The things we do, what we say, how we behave... or take the fickleness of the weather, how we repeatedly change our plans around it, and how amusing our responses sometimes are."

We kept walking in silence for a few moments. Then my mother added:

"Don't take me wrong; life is not a comic strip. It is hard, full of meaningless struggle. But I am seventy years old now and many things don't matter to me anymore, so I can look at them and laugh. That's the advantage of being old."

A British couple stayed in the room next to our's. I could hear them return to their room at 3:00 in the morning, laughing and apparently intoxicated. Tim was a sales manager for Audi, Julian was a homemaker, and they had two young daughters whom they left at home.

"Yes, we're having a *very* good time," Tim replied to my question with a wide grin when I ran into them. He seemed a bit tense, though: "What do you do, Paul?" he asked.

"I'm an economist. Presently, however, I'll be working on a book."

"Oh? What's it about?" he asked the universal question.

"Social psychology. The title is *If Life Is a Game, How Come I'm Not Having Fun?*"

"It's a very interesting question," Julian commented, standing next to Tim.

"Yes. But you, no doubt, are having fun. Life is exciting for you . . ." I responded.

"Oh, no!" Tim smirked. Julian's head shook to and fro hesitatingly. Their eyes shone intensely: "Well, yes, we are having fun, but this is a vacation. Here it is different; this isn't *life*," he added with a subdued voice.

"It was only for three days; we're leaving today," Julian extended an explanation.

Psychologists acknowledge that Sundays, holidays, vacations, and most fun activities fill Americans and Westerners with acute uneasiness and apprehension. A medical doctor told me that more executives have heart attacks on Monday mornings between 7:00 and 9:00 A.M. than at any other time. The medical profession refers to it as "Sunday Neurosis" rather than work apprehension.

Many of us plan our vacations weeks in advance. As the day approaches, we hope that nothing will happen in the interim—like a severe case of the common cold in the family or an emergency popping up at work. And if no unwelcome problems befall us, we get to go away. Then we become anxious about stuff we left behind: the accumulating toil that awaits our return, a possible decline in the business profit due to our absence, the bills piling up during the vacation, or the children we didn't take along so they wouldn't spoil our getaway. At work we are expected to be serious. When we aren't serious, even outside work, we feel guilty.

I cannot help thinking that there has to be a practical way to combine the serious and jovial aspects of our toil, and to get rid of the ideologies that burden us with so much guilt about pursuing joy in our everyday activities.

Let's Play Sisters

Stephen Minot, a professor at the University of California, points out in his widely read textbook how uncertain college students are about whether being *serious* is a perception or a feeling. "There is an unfortunate confusion in the English language," he writes, "between *serious* as a furrow-browed emotion, and *serious* meaning complex or insightful."[11]

Contemporary psychologists describe two basic needs that we humans have: the need to discharge pent-up energy, and the need for emotional experiences. In our culture, as Robert E. Neale put it, work has become a conflict between these two needs, whereas the dynamic of play results in their harmony.[12] It is a natural human necessity. The prominent psychologist Erik Erikson referred to play as "psychological work."

Dr. Gulick reports about two sisters who had been quarreling. To end their contention, one said to the other: "Let's play sisters." From that moment on their relation became harmonious. In deciding to *play* sisters, they chose their relationship. Up to that point they were stuck in it.[13]

Another example offered by Gulick takes place during a visit in Pratt Institute. While on tour there, he noticed that a toolmaker was absorbed in examining the perfection of the fit between two parts of a certain device he had made. Gulick became curious:

"How closely does it fit?" he asked the toolmaker.

"I don't know... closer than one-thousandth of an inch," the toolmaker replied.

"Can't you tell for sure?" Gulick inquired.

"I have no calipers that will register closer than that," explained the toolmaker.

"Is it necessary to fit it so closely then?" Gulick continued his inquiry.

"No."

"Why do you do it then?"

The toolmaker looked at Gulick bewildered. To the toolmaker it was play. He was proud of his work. It reminded Gulick of the old violin-makers, for whom work was also play.[14] According to Gulick, the teacher who loves to teach, the stockbroker who loves to gamble, the business executive who is fascinated by the corporate game, the inventor who forgets to sleep, and the parents who do their tasks with joy born out of love for their child rather than duty—they are all playing.

When my great-aunt Cecile works with patients, she's playing the role of a physician. She's doing a serious and important thing—

she *helps* people. She's fully conscious of the fact that she fulfills the role and expectations of a physician. Yet, she *plays* a role. When we consciously act a role it isn't a mere pretense, because we give our work the most thoughtful consideration and attention to details that it deserves.

The professional opinion is that during the past fifty years the traditional distinction between work and play has been gradually changing in the American culture. If so, like all ideas, it is evolving very slowly. We still treat games as free-time activities that we engage in only outside work, or frivolous activities we use to keep bored children off our backs. Most people I know still have difficulty playing work. Many of us even *work* at their play.

A Historical Snapshot of Our Paradigm

Without play there would be no normal adult cognitive life, no healthful development of effective life, no development of the power of the will.

—Carl Seashore (psychologist)

Ancient religious rites and ceremonies did not develop merely as a means to release excess energy. They served to reenact the lives of the gods. They were the sociodramas enacted by the gods as they were imagined by our ancestors. Theater, music, dance, and sports, all evolved from our ancestors' need to connect with their deities. Originally, the deities represented natural forces and processes of life.

The professional theater, which is familiar to us, began in sixteenth-century Italy and was known as "Commedia dell'Arte." In those days, the actors did not have written scripts, only a general idea of the desired conclusion for the plots, so they made up the dialogue as they went along. Some of them also wore masks. The unmasked performers represented human characters. Masked actors depicted mythological images or exaggerations of human qualities. Music, humor, sports, and social clubs flourished during affluent economic periods, mainly in ancient Greece, the Roman Empire, Italy, France, the Austrian-Hungarian Empire, Germany, and the United States. When the economic conditions in Europe grew more severe, play and humor were used to magnify the harsh external conditions. Consequently, they were banned. As in our own day, play and humor mirrored the current precepts that have occupied and stirred the public.

So the church called for suppression of deliberate play, promising happiness in a world to come instead of in this world. Parents began to inhibit the natural playfulness of their children. Industry and banking started to emerge in the same period as the fervent pursuits of a new social class, the new and upcoming middle class, achieved through bloody political and social upheavals. People began to take themselves, their new symbols and new quests very seriously, although they never stopped relating to each other by acting roles and wearing masks. The paradigm is that of suppressed play. We find this paradigm at work in business, in the military, in politics, in the creative arts, in religion, in schools, and in every aspect of our daily lives.

But the instinct to play struggles to come out, among other reasons because, as Dr. Carl Hosticka once observed: "Everyone needs to feel important." Psychologist Jerome Singer studied the behavior of social clubs in America. One of them is the Society for Creative Anachronism. The members of this national fellowship assume names from the Middle Ages, Renaissance, and Dark Ages. They use these designations in their meetings, correspondence, and newsletter. Their hierarchical ranks also parallel those periods. And they conduct ceremonies in which they ennoble and crown each other, similar to the Elks, Freemasons, the Knights of Columbus, the Knights of Pythias, and probably other secret social societies.

They hold secret rituals, engage in symbols and allegories, employ secret handclasps and passwords, and use special signs and rings, all of which remind Dr. Singer of children's secret games. Singer gives a colorful description of the fully costumed knights taking part in mock battles on the green plains of college grounds. Their garb is carefully designed, he says, and at their banquets one can imagine oneself being transported back in time to King Arthur's dining table in the legendary Camelot of sixth-century England.[15]

A somewhat different American club is the Baker Street Irregulars. Its members are intellectuals, who dress in English costumes from the late nineteenth and the early part of the twentieth centuries, and endlessly discuss nuances of Sherlock Holmes detective cases.[16]

In Italy, on the eastern border of our Western civilization, a progressive elementary school keeps two dressing rooms with trunks full of costumes, just in case a pupil—while studying history or literature—feels like dressing up that day in a historical or mythological outfit.[17]

If we can recognize the paradigm, we can also bring play into the open to intertwine with work, love, and sound thinking.

Four Chords of Mental Health

For many decades the grand taboo in the scientific study of human beings was the subject of sexuality. But the study of play has been even slower to develop. . . . Sexuality became an appropriate subject for scientific study a number of years ago, but I wonder if play is even now wholly respectable. If anthropology is to reach its objective of gaining an understanding of the human organism and its ways of life, I think that play must be studied.

—Edward Norbeck (Rice University)

The suppressed-play paradigm prevents us from perceiving each other as playmates, or considering our telephones, computers, internet, business negotiations, and religious relics as playthings. Our politically correct words are oriented toward *making* and *doing* and do not include *playing*. Sex, for instance, is not *playing around* but about *making* love. While playing is for its own sake, making anything is oriented toward others and must usually pass their approval.

Yet a certain element becomes clearly evident—our age-old need to play. As Robert E. Neale submits so compellingly, play can no longer be conceptualized as diversion from work, but as a constituent process of work. Erik Erikson's definition of play as *psychological work* has great significance for how we can view our ongoing enactment of roles in society in the future.

I would like to leave you now with the following statement, by a psychologist Ashley Montagu:

"The four great chords of mental health are the ability to love, to work, to play, and to think soundly. It is remarkable how closely interwoven each of these abilities is with one another."[18]

7

A Journey's Aim

> *Why is it that no one is excited? I hear people talking in the laundromat about the end of the world, and they are no more excited than if they were comparing detergents.*
>
> —Daniel Quinn, *Ishmael*

At a writers' conference in California, subsequent to reading a few pages from this book, I told my audience that I do not submit that everyday activities must be a game, but I suggested that such an attitude has definite merit. Then I shared the following story, relayed to me in a letter from a reader of *Dear Brotherhood:*

> I was on my way to a job interview in Sacramento, and the Greyhound clerk in San Francisco directed me to the wrong gate. The same happened to three other people. Consequently we missed our bus, and had to wait four hours for the next one. Of course, we were furious. The other three were fretful during our entire halt. Later, on the bus, they told everyone what had happened to us, and we were encouraged by passengers to sue the bus company.
>
> I composed myself. I figured I could take care of my interview once I got to Sacramento. So, I announced that I was against a legal

action because it would only add to the stress in my life. I said that I prefer to handle my life's events as if they are games.

An accomplished author approached me during the break that followed my presentation, to express her support of my theme. She said to me that lately she finds herself thinking along similar lines to my own:

"Increasingly, I see myself as an actress in various dramas," she shared with me. "*Playing life* instead of *fighting life* makes more sense and is far more interesting."

She reminded me of Kathleen Norris, another novelist who asserted that life can be easier than we actually make it.

A local newspaper salesperson called our home on a Monday evening, just as we sat down to eat supper, and asked for me:

"This is Joe from the *Tribune*," he said. "I'd like to ask you a question, Mr. Brenner, knowing you're a busy man."

"Go ahead."

"Do you read the *Tribune*?"

"Sometimes," I said.

"Would you consider a subscription, sir?" he asked.

"No, Joe," I replied. "Now if you'll permit me, I'd like to continue my dinner."

He hesitated, mumbled "thank you," and hung up. And I rejoined my wife at the table.

Since they were running a subscription special, different sales representatives from the *Tribune* continued to call me every evening that week, always around suppertime. On Friday evening it was the young voice of Margaret:

"Mr. Brenner?"

"Yes."

"I'm so glad to speak with you," she produced jovially. "How are you today?"

"Fine. Very nice of you to inquire."

"Of course, sir. We care about you."

"You do? Why?" I inquired.

"I beg your pardon?" she replied.

"Why do you care about me? You don't know me, so you obviously didn't call to inquire about my good health."

"Well, no sir. You're right," she said. "I called to offer you our subscription. It's the last day of our special, and we want to send you a free subscription for one week so you can decide whether or not you like having it."

"I've already turned the offer down four times. I must say, you people are very persistent. You didn't fail to interrupt my dinner the entire week. Since you didn't call to ask me how I'm doing, why did you say that you care?"

"I'm sorry, sir," she muttered. "I only did what my boss told me to do. Can I put you on hold, please?"

Margaret didn't give me a chance to reply. She put me on hold, but a minute later she hung up. I never heard from the *Tribune* again.

Oh, the lives we have lived, the games we played along the way.

Marketing has become our national obsession. Reporters, attorneys, politicians, doctors, even bakers in supermarket deli departments—everyone constantly sells. It seems that not to try to sell something to someone all the time is un-American. And frankly, I do not think it's fun. We have become sales bureaucrats who view human beings as instruments and resources, not as thinking and feeling *people*.

Yes, money is important, but I believe that how we earn it is even more important to our self-esteem and well-being. I found that there is a great letdown in our sense of joy from life, and in our self-respect, as a result of things we do that we are unconsciously apologetic for, or feel guilty about, in the course of our daily work. And to a person who is unhappy, life cannot be fun.

A Conversation with Nisragadatta

If you want to know what a child is, study the child's play. If you want to affect what the child shall be, direct the form of play.

—Joseph Lee

Sri Nisragadatta Maharaj is an aging contemporary sage in India. Once an interviewer said to him:

"I don't like this play idea. I would rather compare the world to a work yard, in which we are the builders."

Shri Nisragadatta replied:

> "You take it too seriously. What is wrong with play? You have a purpose only as long as you are not complete.... But when you are complete in yourself, fully integrated within and without, then you enjoy the universe."
>
> "Do you mean to say that God is just having fun? That He is engaged in purposeless action?"
>
> "God creates beauty—for the joy of it," Nisragadatta said.
>
> "Well, then beauty is His purpose!"
>
> "Why do you introduce purpose?" Nisragadatta suggested. "Purpose implies a sense of imperfection. God does not aim at beauty—whatever He does is beautiful. Would you say that a flower is trying to be beautiful?"[1]

It has occurred to me that many of us simply don't give ourselves *permission* to enjoy life. Some of us go to great lengths to believe in things, and to do things, which make everyone's lives stressful, sometimes miserable. Reading this conversation in Maharaj's autobiographical book, *I Am That*, somehow reminds me of a humorous tale related by Leo Rosten in *The Joys of Yiddish*:

> Two crotchety old men were sitting on a park bench, lost in daydreaming. After a long silence, one of them uttered: "Oy!"
>
> "You're telling me!" the other replied.

Ira is a spiritual motivator and charismatic teacher. His personal growth seminars and inspirational tapes are sold throughout the United States. I hadn't seen Ira for a few years, then we met again at an event that featured him as a guest speaker. After delivering his speech, we filled up our plates and went to sit in a corner to catch up on old times:

"How's your life?" I asked him my usual research question of those days: "Are you having fun?"

He glanced at me cynically:

"I can't have fun," he said with a mouthful.

"Why not?"

"I'm too busy. You know how it is ... work, work, work," he said.

"Ira, you're a motivational speaker. I listened to your tapes; I have heard your talks. They are all about living fully in the moment, in joy. Very inspiring. I thought that your personal life was the same."

"What can I say? This is the real world," he shrugged, his lip twitching nervously: "Too many problems, too many things to do and not enough time to do them. My life is overwhelming."

He staged a smile and resumed eating. I observed his stress and his tiredness. Speechless for a moment, I contemplated a response:

"Look," he added suddenly, "life is a setup; you know that."

As I said, when a person is unhappy, life is not fun. Although Ira is a spiritual leader and makes a living inspiring others to believe in an ideal world, deep down my mother and Ira seem to share a similar worldview. Growing up in a family of Holocaust survivors, it was inconceivable to me that someday I could have a life that is free of worry. In my family, if we didn't have something to worry about, we worried about that. My mother was a perpetually unhappy woman. She didn't like this world because of what people do to each other. She has never felt safe in it. No matter how good things would get, she always anticipates a pending catastrophe. It has caused anguish for all of us. Life for the members of my family has been a compromise, and feeling guilty if we had too much pleasure, our happiness always had to be spoiled by it. My mother even had a trick to avoid gaining weight. She simply told herself that whatever she ate didn't taste good.

For years I believed that unhappiness was necessary in order to survive. Nothing motivates like discontent to work harder and to earn more money. I became a superachiever, and my discontent became my insurance policy. When I later recognized my disposition to continually create stress and anxiety in my life, and my dependence on it to keep on being successful, I decided to change that. But then I encountered another obstacle, inherent in the American capitalistic formula for success. Success is not stress-free. Nevertheless, whether unhappiness is a motivating force or an effect, the result is the same.

Recently my friend Toni, a writer, sent me this e-mail:

> I am a jinx. If I use a certain thing, it breaks. For example, I was the last one to use the washer. It's broken. I was the last one on my computer. It has a virus, and now I have to use another one. Or should I? The toilet was broken. Did I have anything to do with

that since I've been constipated with stress? Who knows. I daren't touch my husband! So, I'll just sit in the middle of the room and read a book—unless the pages go up in flames!

Humor is Toni's way of dealing with stressful situations. Either that, or be perpetually depressed. God knows, there are infinite reasons in modern living why we should be stressed and depressed.

Unfortunately, the traditional repression of play, humor, and wit deeply changed our ability to enjoy life and to be content. It has turned us into severe, aggressive, function-oriented rather than people-oriented, creatures. Being human or humane is mostly a poetic phrase, as the following anecdotes further illustrate.

The Inmates' Revolt

Let us always recall that it is only a game, a form of play.

—Larry Dossey, *Healing Words*

On 28 June 1965, the *New York Times* reported a prison revolt in which two guards were taken hostage by inmates in order to negotiate their escape. The warden declared: "I refuse to make deals at any time; therefore I don't listen."[2]

Six years later, on 9 September 1971, inmates at the Attica, New York, penitentiary took several guards hostage in order to renegotiate poor conditions and racial discrimination in that prison. Again, the warden, supported by Governor Rockefeller, refused to negotiate. Thirty-nine inmates and four guards were killed, and more than eighty were wounded during the police raid. It lasted fifteen minutes.

Someone once said that we tend to create crises because in overcoming them we can become heroes, and find some sense of "purpose." We continually create monsters so that we may slay them.

Negotiations, making deals and compromises, are part of a conscious game. But the two wardens and the governor refused to play, which resulted in a bloody tragedy. While in our personal dramas we are the sole subjects and heros, in the external melodramas there are only objects and no real heroes, and a big price to pay.

A rabbi-friend of mine once told me a yarn:

"Do you know why it isn't kosher to combine dairy and meat foods?" he asked me.

"No, I don't," I admitted slightly embarrassed.

Sacrifices of firstborn animals were customary in the biblical days. The revolutionary Hebrew laws prohibited animal sacrifice. An ordinance disallowing the sacrifice of baby calves says: "Thou shall not seethe a kid in its mother's milk" (Deut. 14:21).

Legend has it, the rabbi told me, that a group of rabbis decided to take up the issue with God. They asked God:

"This divine prohibition means to not cook a calf that still drinks its mother's milk. Therefore, mustn't we keep our meat and milk completely separate in our kitchens?"

"It means not to murder babies for religious rituals," God replied.

"We should probably also build separate washing sinks, to avoid mixing the dishes, God forbid," the enlightened rabbis went on.

"All it means is not to sacrifice animals."

"And we should allow at least six hours between eating meat and dairy," the rabbis, who felt invested in preserving the tradition, elaborated.

"Have it your way!" came the resigned voice from heaven. And that's how the Jewish dietary laws have survived to this day.

There is an old saying that angels can fly because they take themselves lightly; maybe we cannot fly because we take ourselves so seriously. As this tale so vividly illustrates, we tend to be self-complicating. Regardless of our stations and roles in society, more often than not, we read into others' intentions and over-interpret situations, instead of accepting them at their face value or simply enjoying the moment.

In the Royal Gardens of Innsbruck

The persons with whom one has all the time to be serious—the ones with whom one cannot play around, the ones that one cannot toy with and put on—such persons are the ones with whom the relationship is tense, without being at the same time intense.

—David L. Miller, *Gods and Games*

In the Austrian Alps, in the Royal Gardens of Innsbruck my wife and I watched people play chess on large boards painted on the grounds. The youngest player was a teenager, the eldest in his eighties. They maneuvered the massive pieces skillfully, spending long grim hours contemplating their moves while surrounded by silent and tense spectators. They were competitive, although no prize is given to the winners. I was told that these games go on daily, shine or rain or snow.

I studied the facial expressions, the subtle concerns, anticipations and disappointments of the players, and of their soundless onlookers. When I was growing up, we always played *with* each other. Today people play *against* each other.

Today, high-school coaches whose teams don't win are dismissed, irrespective of the wonderful time that the children may have playing, or of the valuable learning experience these games represent. Consequently, pupils who do not qualify as *winning assets* for their teams are not allowed to play. Anxiety rather than excitement is the young athletes' fill.

The educators Cor Westland and Jane Knight are concerned about this issue. They caution us that our competitive culture no longer tolerates the weak, small or mediocre:

> This tendency leads to serious problems of confidence, security and self-esteem. The stress and tensions that surround participation under these circumstances hamper the emotional and social development of those who have fallen victim to this "win at all cost" syndrome.[3]

That opposite every winner must be a loser, is already a cliché. Indeed, one soccer team's gain is another team's loss. Second place no longer counts; we do not celebrate silver medals or "almost winners," and we do not remember vice presidents. When we win, we say that we *beat* our competitors, *kicked* their asses. To "beat" means to hit hard, to strike blows repeatedly to overcome. In war, the arms are artillery and nuclear weapons, where the losers sometimes die. Here, the firearms are money, labor, insensitivity, a thick skin, and the losers are living dead.

Fifty-year-old Jerry went fishing for salmon early on Sunday. Driving back home shortly after noon, Jerry fell asleep at the wheel, causing his pickup truck to collide with a tree. Eleven stitches were sewn in his scalp, and the totaled truck was towed away.

"I couldn't fall asleep the night before, thinking about the fish I would catch at dawn," Jerry told local reporters when he came out of the hospital: "But the worst of it was that I didn't catch a salmon. I trolled around for four hours and didn't even get a strike."

Fishing, like all sports, ought to be a joyous activity. Competitiveness, however, has become a theology in our culture, and we pursue it with religious zeal. We encounter it on the playing field, in the ring, in Congress, on the highway, and even on a solitary fishing excursion. As a sociologist Elliot Aronson put it: "we manifest a staggering cultural obsession with victory."[4] Jerry lamented that the injury to his head and the damage to his truck were in vain because he had not succeeded in catching a single fish. Ironically, for Jerry, the damages would have been worthwhile had he brought home a trophy. Conversely, I believe that enjoying what we do when we do it constitutes the win, with or without getting a strike.

The Competitive Edge

Your friend is lonely because he will die without seeing. In his life he just grew old and now he must have more self-pity than ever before. He feels he threw away forty years because he was after victories and found only defeats. He'll never know that to be victorious and to be defeated are equal.

—Carlos Castaneda, *A Separate Reality*

In *The Social Animal*, Elliot Aronson shared the experience of how his teacher would call on another pupil with a question for which he knew the answer; he hoped and prayed that the other pupil would come up with a wrong response so that Elliot would have a chance to impress his teacher and colleagues with how smart he was: "What people fear when they engage in the struggle is not that they will fail to get their breakfast next morning, but that they will fail to outshine their neighbors,"[5] Bertrand Russell wrote.

On a similar note, let us take a look at sex. Many of us still label sex as "fun," but much of the time it is a performance feat. Some of us intake substances in order to drop inhibition during sexual intercourse, to ensure that they will be able to perform to their partner's satisfaction. Reading a good book or strolling in nature is much more fun than that.

To live more happily, we may have to ease the nearly panicked condition in which our brains operate today. We may have to lessen the pressure or tension that psychological survival places on us. Modern competition makes life very difficult, often overwhelming. However, we are likely to enjoy our competitive pursuits if we treat them as games. We can initiate game rules that will enable us to compete without destroying people's life savings, without threatening each other's jobs, security, and self-worth.

We can learn from observing the dynamics of our body. It is a community of innumerable parts, individual and replaceable. And yet, once an organ is cut out of the body, it can no longer live. That is so because each member receives its life from the entire system. At the same time, when any bodily unit stops functioning effectively, it affects the entire body's operation, reduces the overall efficiency, and sometimes impacts the whole body's chances of survival. Consequently, we find our bodies to be an instinctively compelled obedience. All the members of our body work in complete synchronicity and absolute interdependence, no competition and no envy.

There are no parts that are more important or less popular in our body: The brain serves as a liaison; its duty is to direct information and to coordinate between all units. The mouth is the spokesperson for the entire system, the only voice that represents and expresses the human being's wishes in its interaction with the external world. There is no competition for these or other tasks, nor are their functionaries venerated or worshiped by any of the rest.

Every cell, organ, or limb inevitably has confidence and trust in all of the other members. Each one functions in the most efficient way possible to itself, and thus contributes effectively, and yet effortlessly, to the entire body's operation. A tenet of congenial and compatible existence is fully embraced by every cell, organ, or limb. Loyalties are directed not toward each other, not toward "celebrated" members or units, not toward particular ideologies within the system, nor toward units or philosophies outside the system. All organs are solely committed to the body's congruous operation as a whole. Together they constitute a most competent orchestra that creates a harmonious symphony.

The same model repeats itself throughout the natural world. Every galaxy, every planet, and every abbey operates that way. There is one catch, however. To have a compatible organism, all members must share the same worldview—the I-Am of the system.

Indeed, every member is totally committed to the same perception of life, and contributes its best effort to the order as a whole. In return, each member enjoys a harmonious, struggle-free, worry-free existence. Our problem is uniquely human: a worldview cannot be forced. That is why totalitarianism, communism, and socialism failed everywhere. That is also the cause for the difficulties and insecurities that are inherent in republics, democracies and capitalism. The German philosopher Friedrich Schiller could be right when he suggested that human beings can only be completely human when they play. We may have to learn to live like playmates, rather than continue to survive as multilevel competitors.

Kohn's Case against Competition

Competition—no matter in what amount it exists—is always destructive. This position, even though it sounds radical, is backed by research.

—Alfie Kohn, "The Case against Competition"

Most experts agree that persons who always have to win the day, are not likely to enjoy either their work or their play. Dr. Kohn works with teachers around the country and is a national speaker in education conventions. In his powerful book *No Contest: The Case against Competition*, Kohn reviews what he describes as the four myths of competition:

1. the myth that competition is unavoidable; that it is part of our *human* nature;
2. the myth that competition is necessary because it motivates us to be efficient; that we would cease being productive without it;
3. the myth that competition is beneficial because it builds good character;
4. the myth that competition is fun.

"I have been working on this topic for about seven years," he writes, "and I have not found a shred of evidence to support the common assertion that competition is an inevitable part of 'human nature.'"[6] Rather, he calls it "cultural obsession." He points out that survival of the fittest does not involve competition at all. Survival of the fittest merely suggests that creatures who adapt best to a changing environment are allowed to live and continue to reproduce. He believes that survival demands that individuals work with, rather than against, each other.[7]

Kohn's argument of import is that we actually do better when we work together rather than trying to best each other. Agreeing with Elliot Aronson that "Trying to do well and trying to beat others are two different things," he cites research findings that indicate that competition can be counterproductive. One of his examples is competitive journalism, which frequently leads to hyping the facts and boosting their relevance. The consequence is that we receive distorted information.

As for building good character, Kohn believes that being competitive only cultivates personality traits that are needed for competitiveness. And although one continuously and deliberately develops competitive traits, one still has to psych oneself up every day to do whatever it takes. "Healthy competition" is a contradiction in terms,[8] he says. While losing in competition generates more belligerence in the loser because of the fear of repeated defeat, winning produces in the winner even greater aggression because of the need to continue to succeed. It is fun for neither the defeated nor the victor—hence, everyone loses. The main outcome is general and all-encompassing aggression: "We are brought up not only to compete frantically, but also to believe in competition,"[9] he told a conference on conflict management in Washington, DC, in 1989.

The Meaning of Anxiety

Human beings, whatever their position in society, feel insecure, lonely, and deprived of the naive, simple and unsophisticated enjoyment of life.

—Albert Einstein, *Out of My Later Years*

We live in an age of anxiety. If one penetrates below the surface of political, economic, business, professional, or domestic crises, one runs athwart the problem of anxiety at almost every turn.

—Rollo May, *The Meaning of Anxiety*

Professor Rollo May of Harvard University expresses similar ideas to Kohn's case against competition. He maintains that our collective exhaustion and pervasive anxiety stem from our competitive way of life, and he is credited with coining the term *competitive anxiety*. He is the author of a number of popular books in psychology, one of which is *The Meaning of Anxiety*. In it, he asserts that anxiety is a modern phenomenon that characterizes our own age, and that was entirely absent before the Renaissance period.

According to May, it was during the Renaissance that people began to treat society as a wrestling ring for power. Audacity, force, and unscrupulous dealings began to spread then as requisites for personal success. Governments started to pass rapidly from the hands of one tyrant to another. May refers to Michelangelo, who boasted: "I have no friend of any kind, and I don't want any. Whoever follows others will never go forward!"[10]

During the generations that followed, doubt, skepticism, personal isolation, and apprehension grew. Nowadays, even getting up in the morning is a great cause of stress.[11] Awaking, at dawn, only to realize that one is a human being, a member of society, seems to require a tremendous reservoir of energy. Today both spouses have to work long hours and engage in endless cutthroat competitions. It is curious that as our standard of living rises, we don't become more relaxed, but more ruthless:

"As soon as I return home from work, I must first drink two cans of beer to replenish my energy," Lena, a clerk at a major supermarket chain, shared with me. Over the past few years, I hear more and more from young people—waitresses, taxi drivers, bank tellers, and students—that they get up in the morning already tired, and that this weariness stays with them throughout the day. Some have shown me bags of vitamins that they carry around to periodically boost their energy and to combat their headaches.

Our television programs and magazines are saturated with advertisements for pills for fatigue and head pain, but few ask how come we are burdened by *so much* weariness and so many headaches. With Kohn and May, I believe that these symptoms are produced by competitive anxiety. It leads to panic and results in frantic behavior. Scientists attributed to it many of our modern maladies, our need for such a large number of hospitals, clinics, laboratories, sanitariums, medicines, and books on health, and our preoccupation with healing.

There may be too many of us, and we are agitated because we live in congested communities and constantly invade each other's space. But we have grown hostile because we have become competitive. And as much as we wish to be important, praised, and loved by all, the outcome of our competitiveness and obsession with victory is mutual abhorrence.[12] It leaves no room for natural fun. To cite May, we are like the sheep who constantly expect to be hunted down, or to be electrically shocked in the laboratory. And like the seals, who have to wake up every ten seconds to survey the landscape lest Eskimo hunters sneak up on them. Adopting a playful spirit in everyday life, however, can change all that.

8

Happiness and Bargains

We are unhappy married, and unmarried we are unhappy. We are unhappy when alone, and unhappy in society. We are like hedgehogs clustering together for warmth, uncomfortable when too closely packed, and yet miserable when kept apart. It is all very funny.

—Arthur Schopenhauer (German philosopher)

After Experience had taught me that all the customary attractions of social life are vain and futile—I finally resolved to inquire whether there is a way which would lead me to enjoy continuous, supreme, and unending happiness.

—Baruch Spinoza, *On the Improvement of Understanding*

Success in life can be measured in two ways: either by one's amassed economic, social, or political accomplishments, or by one's demonstrated ability to be happy and content. Traditionally, we resort to the first measure. We have been ignoring the second criterion that marks a successful person—enduring happiness.

There are many people in our society who are neither wealthy, nor famous, nor politically influential, but who are genuinely happy and consequently live by rational principles. I dare say that they are the really successful people in our society, and it is unfortunate for all of us that they do not receive the true credit that is due them as role models. We focus on our material and drug lords instead of on our joy lords.

Since we follow a theory that wealth and fame constitute personal success, our success role models are famous politicians born with charisma, an advantage since the advent of televised elections, who may be actually unhappy or corrupt. Or celebrated entertainers and athletes who are afflicted with long and severe depressions, who do not enjoy playing for the public any longer and who resort to drugs and alcohol to continue to perform. Many of our role models today would be the first to admit that they do not consider themselves successful, while we insist on envisioning them as such.

During the reign of Flavius Domitian, the pinnacle of Roman success was the invitation to appear in the emperor's bedroom before dawn. Rome's most rich and powerful gathered around the emperor's bed before he woke up, watched him get dressed and eat his breakfast, trailed behind him to the reception hall, then stood around and watched him receive official callers and conduct state business. Those who fell out of royal favor stopped receiving the invitation and were no longer considered successful. They often committed suicide because of it.

The Greeks had the answer to life's norm of success. They held that the end of the good life is happiness. Aristotle was very specific, naming happiness as self-fulfillment. According to Ervin Lszlo, who summarized the consensus view of contemporary humanistic thinkers and psychologists, self-fulfillment "is the end of human purposeful behavior.... It is the actualization of any number and any combination of different potentials, according to the temperament and conscious desires of the individual. What is fulfilling for one may be constraining for another."[1]

It is disheartening that so many people in our civilization, to this day, do not pursue happiness. It is equally disturbing that it is so much easier in our own society to be unhappy than to be happy. It seems that we have learned and progressed little in the realm of happiness since the Greeks. By resorting to the wrong measure of success, we ominously mislead ourselves as to the real achievement that is available to us.

Alan is the owner of a successful restaurant I used to frequent. One day, while I was having lunch at his establishment, I asked him whether life has been fun for him. He sat down at my table and poured out his heart to me:

"As long as I have the restaurant, I will not enjoy life. I seriously contemplate selling the business so I can be with my family. I have a son and daughter whom I hardly know. Linda and I have no time for each other; she has her own career. Ironically, I always thought that I was doing it all for all of us, but would you believe that our success, all this money, only alienates us from each other?"

"What do you plan to do?"

"I'll get a job," he said. "But I'll make sure that I have the time I need for myself and my family. The way things are, I keep wondering what life is all about."

All said and done, what most of us truly hope and aspire for is the achievement of a state of contentment, a happy life irrespective of the financial or political recognition we were able or lucky to generate.

There is nothing wrong with having wealth: "Wealth is a sacred thing," wrote the French author Anatole France. *Sacred* is an unfortunate choice of words, but it is certainly preferable to living in poverty. Poverty is a person's worst enemy. It debilitates one's self-respect. It breeds destitution, self-pity, and desperation. It fosters inferior education. Privation distorts reality and sends one spinning in delusions. A solid education and a career in a productive theatre ought to be everyone's plan to overcome poverty.

I know of a perplexing number of individuals who indulge in new-age and risky schemes with the hope of manifesting quick abundance, which only hinders their ability to snap out of perpetual destitution.

We are now witnessing in our country a historically new and totally unexpected phenomenon—the poverty of abundance. Affluence is progress if it improves the standard of living of the entire population of a country. Most of our wealth, however, is concentrated in the hands of families that represent only about 5 percent of the American people. At the same time, a flood of cheap and poor products creates the illusion of abundance, which, in turn, does funny things to people.

It has changed many of us into ardent and ruthless pursuers of cash for its own sake and at all costs. Most of us are no longer shocked when beef growers inject chemicals into cows knowing it can poison people, or when food manufacturers continue to deny the very existence of food-related allergies. We do not boycott car manufacturers that don't recall defective models calculating that it is more cost-effective to pay damages to surviving invalids or families of casualties, because these cars are cheaper to buy than others. Some doctors prefer to prescribe drugs and surgeries in lieu of simple exercise and moderate eating, and we keep swallowing these expensive drugs. Some state courts today even allow politicians to be deceptive in their election campaigns, and we continue to vote for them because they promise us lower taxes. And teenagers complain to their indulgent parents: "You never give me anything!" because they no longer appreciate what they have, and are quick to anger when they don't get what they want. Having more, means less and less. The more we have, the more stressed we get, and the more we complain. A successful stockbroker said recently on television: "Many people are successful today, so it is no longer enough to be rich; I want to be *feared.*"

We have thousands of gurus and spiritual instructors who make their livelihood teaching various kinds of yoga, positive thinking, or meditation. At the same time, we have the world's highest and growing ratio of suicides, teenage crime, mental disorders, hospitals, and asylums. We have landed astronauts on the moon, and we reached Venus. But we have lost our ability to live in happiness on Earth.

"The last of the human freedoms is the freedom to choose one's attitude in any given set of circumstances," wrote Victor E. Frankl, a renowned psychiatrist. We must remember that we can no more stop ourselves from inventing new things than we can halt our ideas. As we grow accustomed to comforts, new amenities are developed that render the old ones obsolete. In a capitalistic system, it is up to each individual to decide when one has enough, when it is time to quit the advertisement game and switch to the game of contentment and happiness.

Successful Executives Pay the Price

Every person who is out for self-betterment with no thought of others, is faced with a host of similarly motivated persons.

—Robert Heilbroner and Lester Thurow, Economics Explained

On 8 August 1996, *USA International* reported that many American executives work fifty-seven hours a week, averaging eleven and a half hours a day. I read somewhere that our hunting ancestors worked one hour a day. One hour a day! We work for money, not for food and shelter, and consequently we buy more things than we need. Surveys show that we end up throwing away more than we consume. And as we saw, the personal bottom line of our *emotional* profit and loss is in the red. That is a mystery that future generations will try to figure out.

In 1996, Chief Justice William H. Rehnquist addressed America's attorneys: "Successful lawyers pay the price," he said. "Many in the profession today work more, earn more, but enjoy life less. There is some connection between the greater number of hours that a typical lawyer puts in today, and the diminishing satisfaction that the profession provides to many who are in it."[2]

During my years as an executive, it was an unwritten expectation that we work long days as well as on weekends. We competed among ourselves to see who stayed later at night and who arrived earlier in the morning. Sixty-hour weeks were common. On the corridor walls hung black-framed photographs of former executives who had died of heart attacks. We never discussed them, nor the pressure, intensity, and uneasiness we always felt. Achievement and social recognition were our crosses to bear: "We are not in this career for our health," we used to say.

According to a survey on the stress of American executives, about a third suffer from anxiety caused by lack of security. In his instructive book *Vital Lies—Simple Truths,* psychologist and best-selling author, Daniel Goleman relates a compelling story about the insecurity of today's corporate vice presidents:

> A particular company had just been swallowed in a hostile takeover by a large corporation. The vice-presidents in the conference room engaged in small talk to cover up their fears of bad news,

while waiting for their senior executive to arrive. One of them shared how worried and vulnerable he once felt when he was asked to change seats during a flight on a small airplane, due to the aircraft's sudden malfunctioning. Another vice-president told about an airplane that caught fire just before take-off, describing in detail the panic that spread among the passengers on board. A third vice-president related how he was caught in sniper-fire while traveling on business to Beirut.[3]

In the end, we are "just trying to stay alive" psychologically and physically, as Gregory Peck said in *The Gunfighter*. We wake up in the morning, and by the inexplicable force of survival and by the will to succeed, we assemble our strength and put on politically correct garments and smiles. And hoping that no one outside will suspect our hidden despair, we come out of the sanctum of our inner worlds and mingle. Driven by blind forces, judges, lawyers, priests, athletes, actors, secretaries, government officials, politicians, college professors, salespeople, factory workers, and cabdrivers continue to dream, plot, and scheme about the fast lane to success.

When evening arrives, we are liberated. We rush out of the offices and factories and hurry through the streets. We dart into our walled houses and apartments and wipe off the smile, exhausted and beaten. Then morning comes again, and we start all over. One is tempted to agree with the German philosopher Arthur Schopenhauer who said that we are encouraged to take our existence so seriously, yet it lingers on the verge of the pathetic. A poem authored by a family friend, Rabbi David Zaslow, echoes the crux of this chapter's theme:

> My Uncle Irving used to say, "You can drop dead any minute.
> And while you are falling to the ground, you've got to ask yourself very quickly,
> Was it worth it? Was it really worth it?
> And by the time you hit the ground, you've got to answer, yes or no.
> If you say *no,* you'll hit the ground like a boulder. Death will be an agony.
> Your life will flash before your eyes, and you'll hate everything you see.

But, on the other hand, if you happen to say *yes*—
You won't even hit the ground. You'll continue falling.
And while your life flashes before your eyes,
You'll feel proud, and wonderful, and complete. It's just that simple."
That's what my Uncle Irving used to say.
Last Passover, my Uncle Irving finished his dinner, got up from the table,
Stretched his arms as if to fly, and started falling to the ground.
He was dropping dead right there, in front of the whole family.
As he was falling I heard him holler, yes! I smiled at his courage.
The last that I heard, my Uncle Irving was still falling.

Kant and the Morality of Unhappiness

For a long time, the question: What makes life worth living? refused to leave me alone. Isn't the ultimate purpose of being alive simply to enjoy it, to be happy in any way we can? On our deathbed, don't we mainly look back to examine whether or not we have been happy? If that is so, why isn't success defined in terms of happiness?

For generations, we have been instructed by the Christian, Jewish, and Hindu religions not to look to earthly happiness, but to some other divine rewards. Theologians and philosophers have been feeling guilty for desiring happiness, and have tried to suppress it. Immanuel Kant, the influential eighteenth-century German philosopher, rationalized it in what he called the "morality of unhappiness." He wrote that the principle of private happiness is the direct opposite of the principle of morality. Happiness should be a consequence, but it cannot be a condition.[4]

The growing secular middle class, however, who became prosperous through the pursuit of capitalism as a means to commercial and political power, rejected the idea of rewards in the hereafter. The modern values that began to emerge gave birth to economics—a new science that focuses on the growth of national wealth. But the underlying assumption has continued to be that human beings can learn to be productive without being happy. An increasingly higher standard of living can also become a religion. Indeed, most economists agree that there is no theoretical limit to the growth of either national or personal wealth. They also agree on the downside—obstructed growth becomes failure. Nowadays, if last month's growth does not get surpassed this month, it is no longer success but failure. Without durable and steady happiness, we, as individuals, are left with nothing to sustain us emotionally.

How "Success in Life" May Be Redefined

A human being cannot wish not to be happy.

—Blaise Pascal (mathematician)

In his *Memoirs*, Elie Wiesel tells the story of a boy, very tall and thin, who thought himself to be already dead. During World War II they were together in a concentration camp. Wiesel narrates:

> "No one will ever convince me that the Germans will let even a single Jew escape alive," he used to say. Granted, he ate and drank, but as he pointed out, "perhaps the dead too, eat and drink as we do." A constant smile hovered about his lips because he firmly believed that the dead were smiling at him. He therefore returned the favor, out of politeness. One evening we were chatting under a tree, and he shared his happiness with me. Yes, that was the word he used: happiness. "I'm happy because I'm not afraid anymore," he said. "I'm not afraid to die because I'm already dead." He is still alive as I write these lines, living in Brooklyn with his wife and children. Those who know him say he believes he's in heaven.[5]

A career, wealth, and a social position in the community can furnish our individual lives with meaning, provided we find genuine pleasure in pursuing them. I believe that what we really hope to find in them is happiness, not the accumulation of success symbols and relics for their own sake. We hope to derive from them contentment.

When I finished high school, I felt that I could not be happy until I finished college. Three years in the army and four years in college, I still wasn't happy. So I went to graduate school. When

I finally stood up to receive my master's degree, all I could feel was inner emptiness. I was devastated. I had worked hard for thirteen years to arrive at that glorious moment, and the only thing I felt was vague pride, no lasting sense of gratification. I thought to myself, I'll surely be happy when I become a corporate executive. After all, wasn't all my studying merely in preparation for that? I became a superachiever, a conqueror of endless battles. Yet as I climbed up the corporate ladder, my contentment seemed to lag behind. Did I have to become the president of General Electric or the secretary of the treasury in order to attain happiness? Would I be happy then?

Most American dictionaries define success as merely "gaining of wealth, fame, rank, etc.," without mentioning happiness, joy, contentment, or peace of mind. I believe that a partial characterization can be misleading and consequently harmful. I prefer the following prescription: "Success in life is personal enduring happiness." My proposed definition asserts that the adage Success Is Happiness is not valid. Rather, Happiness Is Success. As John Barrymore, the accomplished actor, testified, there is a huge difference between achieving to be happy, and happily achieving. My new conceptualization of what constitutes a successful individual reverses the causal relation between personal persisting happiness and one's accomplishments as a role-player in society.

Martin

> When Gloria greeted him at the door her face fell because she, apparently, was expecting someone more handsome, and perhaps taller. During dinner his explanation of how umbrella handles are made just seemed to bore her. And when he tried to charm her with humor, she told him that she really didn't like crude and stupid jokes. At the door, when he tried to kiss her goodnight, she turned her face away and he ended up kissing her barrette. All of that is what happened. He failed *with* Gloria.
>
> —Gary Provost, *Beyond Style*

The novelist Gary Provost's choice of words reflects our cultural sentiment of what has constituted personal success and failure. Obviously there was no chemistry or resonance between Martin and Gloria. It was a match to be avoided. But how can it be considered the *success* or *failure* of either one of them? A healthy and happy relationship is the result of compatible dispositions and temperaments. Seduction and the winning over of members of the other sex are by no rational means an indication of success. Had Martin *succeeded,* using contemporary terminology, it would have been an unfortunate prelude to an inevitable disaster for both himself and Gloria.

Our younger generation finds itself in a difficult bind. On one hand, they are told by school psychologists that their ability to develop skills and to befriend others depends on their being happy. At the same time, they are told by families and teachers that their happiness is a derivative of their ability to compete and outperform others. It is very difficult to transcend this paradox.

Studies show a steady rise in rivalry and competitiveness among five- and-six-year-olds.[6]

One evening our neighbor, the single parent of a ten-year-old, knocked on our door. Handing a catalog to my wife, he apologized for inconveniencing us:

"My boy has to sell these products, to raise funds for his school. Please find something to order. I cannot afford to buy them myself, and I don't want my kid to feel like a 'loser' in his class because other children's relatives can afford to buy this stuff."

Psychologists acknowledge the fact that children's exposure to unfair and ongoing competitive comparisons in school lead to perceptive distortions of reality, inaccurate self-images, and personality maladjustment. Low income, and a timid and shy temperament, can limit a child's comfort zone when he begs neighbors and relatives to buy gift wrapping and candy to support the school. In turn, these children develop a self-perception of inadequacy, which dooms themselves to self-perpetuating unhappiness.

The high school students in our town hung the following poster on the wall of their school: Children Need to Play, Not to Compete. Below it they listed these justifications:

- Competitive activities are neither satisfying nor beneficial to children.
- Competitive activities are psychologically harmful.

- Parents and coaches emphasize competition and winning, unfortunately providing opportunities to place their own needs ahead of children's welfare.

How It Came to Be That We Have Ten Commandments

Happy is the person who learns the wide chasm that lies between one's wishes and one's powers.

—Johann Goethe (German poet)

By definition, to sustain itself, a capitalistic system must create an infinitely growing number of wants and desires in its consumers. Consequently, as Gerry Spence informs us, American corporations spend on advertising more than our entire country spends on education, every year.[7]

Corporate America is aided by the banking industry. A capitalistic monetary system serves as a vehicle for consumers to keep buying, and for companies to keep selling. Let's look, for instance, at what constitutes our "money." The actual amount of cash that banks keep in their vaults is roughly 20 percent of all the actual checks that we collectively issue to pay our bills. The other 80 percent of our spending represents the banks' debts to each other. The money we have deposited in checking and savings accounts is lent to individuals or small companies to expand their purchasing power, and is no longer in the bank's possession. Banks make profits not on our deposits, but on their own debts.

In the event that the required reserves are 20 percent, the banking industry creates an economy five times that amount. The checks we write to each other are IOU paper notes printed by the banks. If we were all to transform our checks to cash, the entire system would collapse overnight. This will not happen, of course, because the banks will close their doors for a couple of days, during which time they will receive new cash from the government to pay us off. The government prints money to keep the banking industry in business, and us spending.

Hence, the monetary system is geared toward developing a perilous appetite in its population *to want it all*. We buy the advertised message "have it all" in the same way that we buy advertised yogurt, ice cream, or burgers. This is the very root of discontent.

It is especially true in the United States. The aggregate savings of American households is the lowest in the industrial world—less than 5 percent of the national gross income, compared with 15 percent in Germany and 20 percent in Japan.

My point here is not to suggest the mortification of our needs. That is not what this book is about, although discrimination and healthy restraint may be effective for enduring happiness. After all, addicts are adept at rationalizing their excessive and destructive self-indulgence. But this is not happiness. As soon as the good feeling wears off, the addict resumes his or her miserable state. Likewise, people who are heavily indebted to credit cards buy ever-larger computers to keep up with internet requirements, or day-trade in overvalued stocks, often fail to see that these are traps that lead to financial calamity. There is a real difference between taking care of true needs and whimsical wants. Most of our cravings are mere notions, deliberately induced by professional marketers.

The blunt words of Professor Raphael Demos of Harvard University address this matter beautifully:

> I have no automobile, and I say to myself that I am deprived of one. So I procure myself a Ford. But a Buick is better than Ford, and I have no Buick, so I get myself one. There is a better car still, the Cadillac, then there is the Rolls-Royce, then perhaps airplanes, and so on ad infinitum. This idea that I am deprived of a good thing, because I do not have it, launches me into a feverish career of acquisitiveness, in which there is no genuine satisfaction, because there is no point of rest. And it is true that a good deal of present day unhappiness arises from just this conception of privation, with its consequent oversweeping ambition.[8]

The following parody about the origin of our Ten Commandments may provide us with an appropriate illustration:

One day, God had an idea that she felt would fill human lives with meaning:

"Hephaestus!" she called to the Egyptian high priest below.

"Yes?"

"I, Ra, your sun-god, came to give your people a new commandment."

"Life is good. Yet we always want more," the priest replied. "What will it do for us, Great Ra?"

"You will no longer steal and rob each other. An excellent commandment for the soul."

The high priest scratched the back of his head: "Stealing is a way of life for us. Therefore, we cannot accept your offer, Great Ra."

"He is honest," whispered God's confidante in God's ear.

"I'll give it to the Greeks," God replied. "Once one of them has it, they will all want it."

When the Greek philosopher Musaeus walked in the garden contemplating, he suddenly found himself in the presence of Zeus:

"I'm here to give the people of Athens a new commandment," God told him.

"A commandment? . . . What does it say?"

"Love thy neighbors as thyselves; do not murder one another. It will make your mortal lives much more sacred."

"No more killing? We cannot accept this commandment," the philosopher said without hesitation. "It will undermine the entire foundation of human civilization as we know it. Without killing there will be no justice. But to maintain Your grace, Oh Zeus, I shall publicly offer at midnight my firstborn son in your honor."

God shrugged.

A few generations passed. Humanity multiplied, prospered, and progressed. God revealed herself to the French dauphin, Marcel:

"I am the goddess of love. I wish to give the French people a gift, in the form of a new commandment."

"We love gifts. What is it?"

"You shall not commit adultery, and shall not covet your neighbor's spouse. Trust me, you shall be much happier without it."

The dauphin was horrified.

"Oh Blessed Mother, coveting is our way of life. We cannot give it up; we will be miserable!"

God backed off. But then she saw Moses wandering in the desert. Her eyes lit with renewed hope.

"This time I'll add show biz, some good drama to make it important," she told her confidante.

"Moses, Moses!" God's voice resounded out of the fire in the midst of dry rocks, taking him by surprise.

"Who is it?"
"I am JHVH, the God of your ancestors."
"Oh?"
"I heard your people complaining. I came to give them a commandment to cheer them up," she explained.
"The people work too hard," Moses lamented. "The beef is abundant but expensive, and sex has never been better, but who has time anymore? How much will your commandment cost us?"
"Nothing, Moses. It is free."
"FREE? We'll take ten!"

Stretching Up Hands into the Mist

Towards the top the great army thins. On the heights only a few remain, stretching up hands of longing into the mist.

—Will Durant, *The Mansions of Philosophy*

There may be important lessons here. In the eighteenth and nineteenth centuries, the newly emerging middle-class intelligentsia felt guilty for desiring happiness, and gave us the idea that it is unattainable. They replaced their sense of well-being with a series of pursuits, called their achievement "ultimate success," and formed ideologies to back them up—wealth, accumulation of stuff, political power, fame, social influence, sex, individualism, and being feared. When these things fail to bring peace of mind, people are faced with midlife crises. The term *midlife crisis* describes a phenomenon that didn't exist in former centuries. We inherited a miserable quest for happiness.

Pythagoras believed that to secure happiness we ought to resort to conscious *moderation* in all things: moderation in desires, sense pleasures, physical activity, work, rest and sleep, and in goals. All in all, he advocated, happiness lies in moderation and a healthy balance between our pursuits.

Alexander the Great and Napoleon Bonaparte would undoubtedly have been happier, and more successful, had they not desired to rule the world. Both admitted this at the end of their lives. In our own era, the obstacles to personal happiness are complex and numerous. They are steeped in our economic, political, and social structure. They are entrenched in our traditions, perceptions, and worldviews.

I therefore redefined "success in life" as personal enduring happiness. Without happiness people cannot perceive life as fun. Meanwhile, we see that those individuals who do not take themselves seriously, who play life as if it is a game, are happier. *It is not the other way around;* it isn't that people who are happy view life as a game, but people who live as if their lives are a game seem to be happier. Happiness is a state of perpetual contentment, which remains independent of the nature of our games and the results of our pursuits.

After all, a game is a game. The spirit of play is an attitude. All our pursuits, without distinction, may be exhilarating and gratifying when they are approached and viewed as games. The secret to enjoying life lies at the level of understanding.

Part 3

Joyous Minds

For the philosopher Xenophon, the ability to play while preserving a serious frame of mind is accounted as a thing of high value in the art of fashioning life.

—Hugo Rahner, Man at Play

If play is truly a method of self-expression, a communication of goodwill in an inhibited aggression, an important piece in the mosaic of a well-rounded life, then it is indeed a preventive device and a necessity, not a luxury. We lean to the belief that people should play more—not less, and this is in the interests of mental health and the furthering of social good.

—Karl Augustus Menninger

9

The War Games Nations Play

> *We all have secrets we choose not to reveal. One such secret many of us share has to do with war. Officially we're opposed to it. The cliché is that it's hell. But whenever someone extends an invitation to fight, almost everyone accepts.*
>
> —Stephen Minot, *Three Genres*

In one of his famous cartoons, Bill Watterson depicts a young boy asking a stuffed tiger:

"Doesn't it seem like everybody just shouts at each other nowadays?"

The stuffed tiger shrugs it off:

"I think it's because conflict is drama, drama is entertainment, and entertainment is marketable."

Along with money, religion, and the supernatural, wars have been one of the most popular games throughout history. Among other reasons, people go to war for the excitement. Just as religion is a game, and alcoholism is a game, war is also a game.

There hasn't been a single century during which wars did not rage in Europe, as well as in the other regions of the world. During the second half of the twentieth century, there has been a growing antiwar and antimilitarism sentiment in the industrial democracies. Nonetheless, wars, and the political use of war, have not declined. History speaks louder than poems. More than one hundred and fifty wars were fought since World War II. Practically, World War III took place already in terms of casualties; an estimated 7.2 million people died in these one hundred and fifty wars, all of which took place among countries who have been active members of the United Nations. According to Alvin and Heidi Toffler, only three weeks between 1945 and 1990 were war-free.[1]

Americans' aversion to the use of American troops overseas may reflect a lingering post-Vietnam "syndrome." Professors Charles Kegley Jr. and Eugene Wittkopf assert that "American attitudes toward war are episodic rather than steady."[2] According to a 1998 survey, 74 percent of Americans favor U.S. attacks against terrorists, and 57 percent favor participation of American troops in UN peacekeeping deployments to war-torn regions of the world. Only 20 percent of Americans are opposed to war.[3]

War is politics, using a phrase by Donald Snow and Eugene Brown. Countries go to war to procure some political objective they could not achieve in any other way. One of the main reasons for having and using power in American foreign policy, for instance, is to obtain, and maintain, global hegemony. Winning wars leads to favorable economic and political concessions not attainable otherwise.[4] Therefore, it would be erroneous to ignore the war game in this book, which addresses the modern human experience.

Much has been written about the atrocities of battle. I would like, however, to approach combat and the military environment with a different slant, fully aware of the fact that politically I may be stepping into a mine field. With John Garnett, I am not interested in "mad wars," or acts of madness. There is another side to war, as Winston Churchill said during the most atrocious war in European history: War is more exciting than politics. And in war, you can be killed only once, while in politics you can be killed many times. War is a game that should be played with a smile.

War is multifaceted. It is both horrifying and fascinating, the basic emotional conflict that is common to many forms of entertainment. War is typically characterized as a conflict between the forces of good and evil. When a former enemy becomes an ally, and a former ally becomes the enemy, the roles of Christ and Antichrist merely switch role-players.

Many novels, films, television series, and magazine articles, when they are not about outright warfare, are about intense conflicts between individuals. The awesome number of the dead among our fictional characters and heroes surpasses reality. Sometimes I walk away from a movie thinking that unconsciously we may be harboring a collective death wish.

Jerome Singer tells us about a number of American organizations who get together regularly to recapitulate historic battles, using toy soldiers. They dress up in military uniforms from the Civil War or the American Revolution periods. The members of a New York group reenact Napoleon's campaigns over and over.[5]

To assert that we are about to stop all wars in the world is rhetoric. Peace is not the only thing people value; people also want open markets and human rights. Immanuel Kant remarked that perpetual peace is only available when one reaches the final stage, in the graveyard.[6] At the same time, we dread the dark side that war brings out in many of us, yet we are attracted to the game aspect, thrill of combat, and the economic and political advantages obtained through military superiority.

Nevertheless, if armed conflicts were to be played as games, their atrocities perhaps would diminish. Therefore, I may be able to offer a new way of thinking about war and peace. The epic *Mahabharata* deals, on the outset, with the battle between the external forces of evil and righteousness. Written by Vyasa, an Indian sage in the fifth century B.C., this complex poem is really about the ongoing struggle between the internal powers that clash within every human being. Vyasa's premise is that any war fought in the world is merely a projection of a battle experienced within ourselves. Our inner fights almost never cease; it is just that we are so used to living with them, that we do not view them as we do external wars.

My purpose here is not to moralize for or against war, and it has nothing to do with my genuine empathy with victims of war crimes and atrocities. Let's face it: McCarthy's campaign was a civil war. So was the political crusade against President Bill Clinton. What goes on in our courtrooms are terrible wars. On the other hand,

John Kennedy and Russian premier Khruschev were playing a game during the Cuban missile crisis. So were Napoleon and the British general Wellington at the Battle of Waterloo. War games come in different forms. Most skirmishes are bloody whether they are fought on the battlefield, in the courtroom, or on the floor of Congress. Today, psychological survival is as important to individuals as physical survival.

Acknowledging the fact that wars are also games would enable governments to create new rules they will be familiar with and abide by, thus avoiding the anarchic nature that gives rise to war crimes and atrocities. Games are enjoyed, at the very least, because they are played by clear and accepted rules.

A Game Bigger than Life

The strongest and highest Will to Life does not find expression in a miserable existence, but in a Will to War, a Will to Power.

—Friedrich Nietzsche

Toward the end of the 1967 Six-Days-War, the Egyptian soldiers left their belongings and weapons, even shoes, and fled. From horizon to horizon, the yellow sand of the Sinai Desert was covered with trails of abandoned shoes. The pursuing Israeli soldiers took color photographs of the shoes, as well as of the scattered bodies. We fought with Uzis and cameras. The picture-taking symbolized our aliveness, not their death. We were thrilled in the dust and dirt of the desert, glad to be alive.

In *War*, a splendid poem by Robley Wilson, a contemporary American poet suggests that in spite of all the things we say against war, we harbor a secret admiration for the glories of war and cherish historical war heroes. Sometimes they wanted to go to war to turn flames in people's hearts. Names like Alexander, Genghis Khan, Caesar, and Napoleon dazzle us. And since time began, a hundred lovers have camp-followed conquerors, he adds.[7]

The poet has courageously expressed the kind of ambivalence toward war that is shared by many of us. We like to watch military parades and participate in military ceremonies. Our children collect war toys. We love to watch battle movies, read combat novels, and play war games. And we daily, and lavishly, support violent athletes and sports. Our libraries are filled with volumes that are saturated with descriptions about the excitement, strong sense of identity and comradeship, hope of glory, expectation of heroism and patriotism, and personal healing, which took place during war. These volumes are filled with humanity's most powerful stories about people's abilities and might against all perceivable odds, as well as agonizing defeats, which, nonetheless, have not destroyed us.

For the celebrated French artist Fernand Leger, World War I was an occasion for loyalty and solidarity. For Americans like Clancy Strock and Deb Mulvey, World War II was "a time that united all Americans like never before, or since."[8] Strock is a magazine editor. In 1993, he wrote about his experience in the Pacific during World War II:

> It sure wasn't anything like home.... You were a hero even if you had never heard a shot fired in anger. Families adopted you. Young ladies were eager for your company. Everyone was anxious to get to know these strange young men from across the water. Were we really cowboys? Or gangsters? Or movie stars? What an experience! That's not to say that there wasn't mud and rain and cold and terror and close friends who would never come home. That came later. That was war. But for those who did come home, the experiences that went with being overseas left us with a lifetime of memories.[9]

Clandestinely, men and women alike, we love the adventures of war. Traditionally, boys were encouraged to become interested in hunting and fishing, and to join the army, to prove a strong character. Today, women take a growing part in these activities as well. Not because they have to, but because they want to. According to Mulvey and Strock, more than 300,000 American women volunteered for service during World War II. They were pilots, flight instructors, airplane mechanics, marines, nurses, journalists, air traffic controllers, entertainers, secretaries, and drivers. Name it, they did it, and earned the respect and admiration they deserved.[10]

The Civil War has given us our most lovable heroes—Gen. Robert E. Lee; "Stonewall" Jackson; Presidents Abraham Lincoln and Ulysses S. Grant; and Gens. Sherman and Sheridan: "No other chapter in our history has contributed so much to our traditions and our folklore,"[11] writes Henry Steele Commager, a history professor from Columbia University. Edmund Clarence Stedman, a soldier in the Civil War, wrote to his mother:

> I have enlisted all my humble energies in this cause for two reasons: First, the necessity for personal shaking-up and rejuvenating—the old, healthy love for action rising in me, love of adventure, etc. . . . Second, one of principle. Now, for the first time, I am proud of my country and my grand heroic brethren. The greatness of the crisis, the Homeric grandeur of the contest, surrounds and elevates us all.[12]

Commager cites the following story from the *London Times*, written by a journalist who witnessed the battle near Bull Run during the American Civil War:

> Through the wavering mists of light blue smoke and the thicker masses which rose commingling from the feet of men and the mouths of cannon, I could see the gleam of arms and the twinkling of bayonets. On the hill beside me there was a crowd of civilians. A few officers and some soldiers moved about among the spectators, and pretended to explain the movements of the troops below. The spectators were all excited, and a lady with an opera glass, who was near me, was quite beside herself. Such cheers as rent the welkin! The Congressmen shook hands with each other and cried out: "Bully for us! Bravo! Didn't I tell you so?" And the Irish hurrahed wildly. . . .[13]

Every year we celebrate both the Civil War and the War of Independence. Veterans also commemorate the Vietnam War each year. The political scientist Alan Cassels believes that between the French and Industrial revolutions, the former has had a stronger impact on the industrial societies. The French Revolution, a war fought in the name of ideology, changed Western civilization to what we know it to be today: participatory democracies.[14]

Acclaimed philosophers like Hegel and Kant posit that war reinstates nations' moral health. In Kant's words: "a prolonged peace favors the predominance of a mere commercial spirit, and with it a debasing self-interest, cowardice, and effeminacy, and tends to degrade the character of the nation."[15] The 1990s, since the end of the cold war, can attest to that. Friedrich Hegel expressed a comparable view:

> Just as the blowing of the winds preserves the sea from the foulness that results from a prolonged calm, so also the corruption in nations would be the product of prolonged, let alone perpetual, peace. In peace, civil life continually expands, all its departments wall themselves in, and in the long-run men stagnate. As a result of war nations are strengthened. And people involved in civil strife also acquire peace at home through making wars abroad.[16]

Ronald Steel, a contemporary political scientist, stipulates along similar lines:

> As we have left the Cold War behind us, so have we left the American century. The war gave us a sense of purpose, and without it we feel trapped by domestic troubles from which we can find no escape in parades, drum rolls, and demonstrations of resolve. The self-confidence that has always been one of our most attractive national characteristics has been sapped, leaving our nation confused and even embittered.[17]

When the famous Yom-Kippur War broke out in the Middle East, in 1973, I volunteered again to help Israel's fight for survival. Thousands of young American men and women spent days and nights at the international airport in New York, eating cold sandwiches and slumbering in sleeping bags, waiting for an opportunity to volunteer and fight. Nothing makes the human soul soar like the epoch of war. I say this from direct personal experience. People's hearts—not merely their hatred—are expressed more intensely in wartime. Courage, leadership, teamwork, loyalty, love, bonding, and religion become much more resolute.

I was asked to supervise the American airlift to the Israeli fronts. At its beginning, the airlift was a secret operation. I was given a code name and temporary identity as a retired U.S. Air Force officer, and I received daily instructions over the telephone from the Pentagon. Each night, soldiers loaded crates of ammunition, medicine, and food into unmarked carriers, without knowing the nature and destination of the cargo. All commercial telephone lines to Israel were blocked. I was able to contact Israel through the military network, and learned from my father that my mother was on the Egyptian front line as a volunteer nurse, also looking for my missing brother. He switched regiments after he lost his own during action in the Sinai desert, and was later found intact.

Since this adventure took place during my last term at Rutgers University, a Jewish professor lowered my final grade for his course to penalize me for my absence and supposedly to demonstrate his impartiality toward the cause. The other professors gave me my actual grades. But an Egyptian professor exempted me from the final exam in his course, and gave me an *A* based on my previous track record with him. And he was the supposed enemy. Later I received a letter of apology from the Jewish professor.

To better understand the likeness between war and play, we must put aside cultural biases, and try to grasp both war and play for what they are: "Ever since words existed for fighting and playing, men have been wont to call war a game,"[18] wrote Johan Huizinga. A current U.S. government recruitment pamphlet describes war in poetic terms—"crashing through dense thickets in the dead of night, zeroing in on your target with a laser range finder and seizing the objective."

Native Americans played war games regularly. Real danger only lent zest. But because it was a game, their aim was neither to kill nor to conquer. They felt disgraced if they lost even a single man in the attack, and it was common that they would let the enemy get away rather than lose lives. It was a glorious way to resolve disputes. A comment by the anthropologists John W. Loy and Graham L. Hesheth is worthy of note: These war games brought glory to a tribe only when they were played by the rules.[19] "Mad wars" are in fact spectacles of agony. But wars played out by rules similar to those of the Native Americans may be appropriate, moral, and rational games to resolve modern disputes.

In addition, the technological and information revolutions may change completely the nature of future wars, as Professor Steven Metz of the U.S. Army War College has proposed:

> Instead of using explosives to kill and destroy, the warrior of the future might fight with a laptop computer from a motel room, attacking digital targets with strikes launched through fiber-optic webs

in order to damage or alter enemy information infrastructure and data resources.... Hacking, virus-writing, and crashing data information systems—as well as defending against enemy hackers and virus writers[20]—may become the form of future wars.

Elements of Adventure

To play is to participate in an event that takes place by chance, entails risk, and is of remarkable purport.

—Robert E. Neale, *In Praise of Play*

According to Will Durant, Napoleon Bonaparte was happiest when he was on the battlefield, because "there is a joy in danger," using Napoleon's own words. Napoleon loved the excitement, ecstasy, and glory of combat more than anything.[21] And "to Attila and his hordes, their incursion into Europe was an enjoyable episode, diversifying the monotonous round of a pastoral life,"[22] as attested by Alfred North Whitehead, the notable American philosopher and mathematician.

A conscious awareness of the odds of getting killed in war has been but a slight deterrent for millions of soldiers, officers, doctors, nurses, engineers, and reporters, who prefer "the thrills of passion and courage, of imagination and enthusiasm,"[23] which abound on the battleground. To many people, risk is a fundamental element of adventure. Countless individuals sacrifice their material pursuits gladly and enthusiastically for the sake of participating in war.

Dr. Neale names three elements that constitute an adventure:

1. risk;
2. thrill of the unexpected;
3. a significant event.

All three elements exist in wars. According to Neale, wars and mountain climbing have a great deal in common:

In the climbing of a mountain, a life may be lost. The adventurer knows this full well. His or her trust is not in a naive promise of successful outcome, but in the value of an adventure for its own sake.[24]

Psychologist Michael J. Apter reports that when a newspaper predicted an earthquake in New-Madrid, Missouri, on 3 December 1990, people arrived from all over the country to be there in the midst of the earthquake. Many people find dangers irresistible.[25]

Gambling and the stock market, and espionage and police work, are characterized by a clear and present danger. People love the horror rides in Disneyland because they are exhilarating. The thrill of roller coasters, and the hysteria of rock concerts, are forms of exhilaration and excitement that wars provide more abundantly. For a soldier who parachutes during training or battle, or for a performer who jumps from an airplane before an audience, whether or not it is play depends solely on that individual's personal attitude.

In the Armed Forces

When I was asked to write a book on the psychology of play, I remembered a cartoon of a hapless couple on an Aldermaston peace march whose child refused to go with them unless allowed to hold a vicious-looking toy-rocket.

—Susanna Millar, *The Psychology of Play*

The armed forces are among the largest employers in most nations around the world. They employ intellectuals, scientists, doctors, attorneys, and clergy—of all creeds, colors, ages, and sexes. The Pentagon is the largest single agency of the federal government. Before the cuts of 1990, it employed three million people—two million in uniform, and one million civilians in a variety of roles. Since the end of the cold war, their numbers were reduced by the Clinton administration by some 25 percent.[26] The military recruits some of the most intelligent, physically gifted, and ablest graduates of our colleges and universities.

What draws so many talented young people to work for the military? More money is being made working for multinational corporations. Greater fame is being attained in Hollywood, in the media, and in sports. Power and influence are pursued in politics. But the armed forces are still the most dramatic and exciting environment to work in. For many employees in the military, daily work consists of war games—training for action behind enemy lines, or creating war strategies on virtual, computer-simulated full-scale battlefields whether on air, sea, or land.

Military uniforms, ceremonies, ribbons, and medals are relics of a supremely melodramatic nature. The daily formalities of conduct in the military may be likened to a religious ritual: employees salute rather than shake hands, and communicate in their own unique jargon even when they are off duty. Burials are "show business" events with bagpipes and Scottish kilts. And aging veterans, long years after retirement, draw together every year, wearing their wrinkled uniforms, caps, and medals, and proudly salute their flags and each other.

Yes, it is the politically correct thing to say that we hate wars. Meanwhile, we continue to write many more books about all types of war than we do about peace and harmony. How many films are being produced about peace activists, and how many about soldiers, spies, and terrorists? How many movies and television series are not saturated with fierce shoot-outs and reeking killing scenes? All the while, the warrior drumbeat in *Riverdance,* and the sharp warlike motions of its dancers, have captured millions of Americans like a storm. And looking at any *Yellow Pages* under "attorneys," we find the largest number of full-page ads of civilian soldiers for hire, soliciting patronage for their ruthless fighting skills.

Unfortunately, "strife is as real a fact in the world as harmony,"[27] according to Alfred North Whitehead. The question, what makes us heartless and vicious, has occupied the mind of many a writer. Will it ever be possible to resolve our collective death wishes, atrocities, and holocausts?

Three opposing theories have attempted to explain what makes us that way: That we are born evil. That we are born neither good nor evil, but are easily manipulated by our culture and fads. And, that we are inherently both good and bad, hence prone to both benevolent as well as atrocious extremes. Ever since the sixth century B.C., all three propositions have been endlessly and zealously debated, and are still the subject of continuous study.

On the Theory That We Are Genetically Evil

The positive insanity and barbarity of wars, causing devastation and ruin, has no kind of justification. Yet these forms of violence continue, and are supported by the very people who see their uselessness, injustice and cruelty, and suffer from them.

—Leo Tolstoy

According to the first theory, all human beings are born evil and must be tamed and civilized through the education process. Evil is as natural and inevitable as inequality and strife. Our destructive nature, according to this theory, indicates that our goodness is a facade, a sophisticated pretense that serves to promote personal gain. Self-righteousness is a fictitious and deceiving display in some, and self-denial in others. The first siblings in Western mythology, Cain and Abel were already driven by jealousy and rage. It turned them into each other's enemies, resulting in Abel's murder at the hands of his only brother.

In nature too, trees kill other trees; plants kill other plants; and animals kill other animals—for preservation of self, territory, or natural resources. Killing appears to be the basic way of life for all living things.

On the Theory That We Are Born Tabula Rasa

Man is wicked not because he is born so, but because he is rendered so . . . Man is almost everywhere a slave . . . everywhere he sees vice and crime applauded and honored, and so he concludes that vice is good.

—Baron Paul D'Holbach (French scholar)

The second theory holds that human beings are born neither good nor bad, but we follow cultural fads and can be led to destruction by social norms. Values and behavior are determined by "culture," not by free will. Every astute politician, clergy, and business executive knows how to bend the will of the masses to their goals. Our environmental conditions, upbringings, and indoctrination determine our individual temperament and make us susceptible to the idea of violence. That is why people take their religious relics to war, and kill gorillas in Africa to cut off their hands and heads for ashtrays and trophies. According to this theory, these people merely respond to social standards and customs.

According to Eric Fromm, the prominent psychologist, our ancient ancestors were relatively peaceful beings, who, twenty to forty thousand years ago had few wars if any, and who rarely killed each other. Only during the last ten thousand years have wars and atrocities gradually developed and worsened, mostly in the last four millenniums. If chimpanzees had psychologists, Fromm says, they would not be writing books about aggression.

Dr. Fromm believes that humanity has developed its own aggression deliberately, specifically in order to create and fight wars. It took a great cumulative effort for religious and political institutions over thousands of years to convince people to fight, against their natural instinct to flee, hide, or submit. It required an incredible amount of ideological indoctrination to suppress people's flight instinct; to make them believe in "honor" and to obey their king and country for fear of being called a "coward," a "traitor," or a "heretic"—a fear that has become greater than the fear of death.

In short, according to Fromm, it took a long time for humanity to develop war as a cultural phenomenon, and to expect adventure and fun from it. In 1914, thirty-nine internationally acclaimed German scientists, philosophers, clergy, artists, poets, and jurists advanced this theory by signing the famous "Manifesto to the Civilized World" on the eve of World War II. In that public manifesto, they claimed: "It is not true that opposition to our so-called militarism does not constitute opposition to our culture, despite the hypocritical allegations of our enemies. . . . Anyone who opposes German militarism, necessarily opposes German culture as well."[28]

On the Theory That We Are Genetically Both Good and Evil

It is almost impossible systematically to constitute a natural moral law. Nature has no principles. She furnishes us with no reason to believe that human life is to be respected.

—Anatole France (French writer and Nobel laureate)

The third theory maintains that there is no such thing as either a good or bad human nature; that we are born good and evil, and therefore capable of both. Since both good and evil exist in the natural universe, they are both natural and inherent aspects of the external world in which we are forced to function. Inside our inner worlds, some of us may not like it, but we are faced with it in the outer world, finding ourselves not only in the midst of evil but also acting it out.

Freud posited two simultaneous instincts in humans: the instinct of life, Eros, and the instinct of death. That is to say, as there is in us a will to live, there is in us also a will to die. This, according to Freud, translates into a constant play between love and hate, pleasure and risk, and a concurrent attraction to life and death. It may explain why so many historical and fictional heroes were also ruthless killers—King David, Alexander the Great, Wyatt Earp, Jesse James, Robin Hood, and *licensed to kill* James Bond. When the instinct of death is directed against ourselves, it becomes a self-destructive drive. When this instinct of death is directed outward, we kill and torture other living beings.

This theory strives to explain why we are at times good, at times cruel, and at times ambivalent. Why we are compelled to commit atrocities, to rob, to rape a child, to murder, and to mutilate—things that a species whose nature is only good could not do. And why those who act so atrociously against other people and animals also often demonstrate strong compassion for babies, people, and pets.

Without going into the supernatural debate, these are, briefly, the three most adhered-to theories about human nature.

Lessons from the Holocaust

> I "understand" the savagery of the Germans, for savagery was their "vocation," their politics, their ideology, their education. But what about the others? The Ukrainians who beat us, the Russians who struck us, the Poles who humiliated us, the Gypsies who slapped us, the Jewish kapos who clubbed us? Why? To show the killers they could be just like them?
>
> —Elie Wiesel, *Memoirs*

If people didn't take themselves and wars so seriously, winning wouldn't be as important as making a point. If we played warfare as we do football or boxing, by a rule that permits no torture, and that allows death only on the scene of battle, we could eliminate war atrocities.

We lose ethical boundaries; we become dehumanized, because we consider life, ourselves, leaders, country, relics, and slogans so important and crucial. That is when things go too far.

Ironically, the Holocaust did create an exceptional race—certainly not that of the Aryan people, but that of the Jewish people. The effort to eliminate the Jews intensified their survival-of-the-fittest process. While many of the physically and psychologically weakest Jews perished, many of those who survived did so by virtue of their physical strength, shrewdness, and psychological survival skills. The process has produced a more resilient race, as is evident in the high visibility of post-Holocaust Jewry in various roles and theatres—from leading scientists to politicians and entertainers.

Perhaps the most shocking aspect of the Holocaust is that it was carefully premeditated, meticulously documented, and methodically executed. Two motivating factors stand out from the research I have done on the subject, underlying the Holocaust, the Christian Inquisition, and America's McCarthyism:

1. indiscriminate patriotism;
2. widespread dread in the population, created through intimidation by the elite.

A sweeping sense of patriotism and widespread fear, together, can create whirling masses that no one may be able to control. This emotional whirlpool drags everybody into a rapid spin, and destroys everyone and everything that gets in the way. That is how common people end up doing such terrible things to one another in the name of ideologies, concepts, and symbols—be it God, king, country, democracy, communism, or capitalism. Because they appeal purely to passion, they often turn people away from reason and moral discrimination.

The following study, conducted after World War II by Stanley Milgram, an American psychologist, demonstrates the impact of authority on people:

> The participants were volunteers. A university professor in a white laboratory coat carrying a clipboard, monitored the experiment. The volunteers, informed that they were taking part in a research project aimed at determining the effects of punishment on learning, were told that there were students in the next room who were tested on memorized lists of data. The volunteers' task was to push a button that administered electric shocks to the tested students whenever a

student made an error. As the test progressed, the jolt was gradually intensified. Soon the volunteers began to hear sounds of increasing pain and anguish.

Although in actuality the other room was empty, the volunteers didn't know that the voices which they heard were not real. As the cries and pleas to stop the shock treatment heightened, some volunteers expressed anxiety about continuing the project. But when the professor in the formal white coat said matter-of-factly that it is a very crucial study, and therefore they must continue to administer the electric shocks, most of them did.

I propose that if the volunteers treated the whole thing as a game rather than as a very important "anything," they would have stopped the test at the first sign of inflicted pain. A playful spirit would have kept them humane. Play reduces social distance between individuals, using the phrase of Robert Fagen, the famed naturalist. Playfulness develops intimate social bonds that approach what some humanists may call "love."[29]

Hence, conducting wars with a playful spirit may enable participants to enjoy the adventure, thrill, comradeship, and acts of heroism that wars inspire, without slipping into atrocities.

The Elephant and the Fly

Governments are far too dependent on the economic beneficiaries of the war machine, to expect from them a decisive step toward the abolition of war.

—Albert Einstein

Many leaders, political scientists, and contemporary scholars believe that under certain circumstances wars are still justified, even though they may inflict pain on a few, as long as they serve the interests of a majority. After World War I, Henry Ford declared that there will *never* be another war in the world. He rationalized that "people are becoming too intelligent ever to have another big war."[30] But in a poll conducted during the depression of the 1930s among nineteen thousand American clergy, almost half of them said that they *would* participate in another war.[31] At the beginning of World War II, Franklin D. Roosevelt announced to the world that the United States would remain impartial, but he sold arms, food, clothing, and medicine to the Allied troops. Our neutrality meant business that was badly needed after the economic depression of the 1930s.

Since the collapse of the Soviet regime in 1989, and with it the breakdown of the economic stability and security of the Russian masses, regional wars have continuously erupted in the former provinces of the Soviet Empire. In 1990, shortly after the cold war ended, we faced economic recession. In January of 1991, President George Bush quickly mobilized land, sea and air forces, and sent over half a million American troops, in addition to two hundred seventy thousand from other Western countries, to start the Persian Gulf War.

In their excellent book, *War and Anti-War*, Alvin and Heidi Toffler narrate the story of Don Morelli, the forty-nine-year-old American general who, while dying of cancer, created the brilliant strategy that was implemented in the Gulf War against Iraq nine years later.[32] In one theatre, diplomats negotiate peace. In another theatre, soldiers and scientists prepare for war. That is how the game is played. As secretary of state, Warren Christopher, said in October 1996: "The lesson of our time is that we must combine force and diplomacy when our important interests are at stake.... There is no doubt that we will use force when we must."[33]

A fly cannot stop an elephant even if it sits on the elephant's back.

Riding the Roller Coaster

The fiery and destructive passions of war reign in the human breast with much more powerful sway than the mild and beneficent sentiments of peace.

—Alexander Hamilton

Oceans storm; fires storm; our minds storm. It is nature's nature to storm. But there is no anger in nature's stir, no frustration, and no hatred. Amity and tranquillity underlie its depth. When the wavethrusts end, the torrent retreats. The earth does not counterattack with feelings of hurt, pain, or vengeance. Peace then envelops both ocean and land. Harmony and balance are reinstated in nature.

The Black Death consumed half of Europe's population in the fourteenth century. It happened again in the sixteenth and seventeenth centuries. Viruses like smallpox have killed more people than human warfare, in their own effort to survive. It is never personal—it lacks spite, vendetta, punishment, or hard feelings.

Have you watched war games that puppies play, or that dogs and cats play, or birds, or lions? They are seldom bloody. Animal behaviorists tell us that animals are extremely careful not to hurt each other when they play. They rarely kill, and hardly harm each other during play, except by accident. To some of us, their games may appear vicious, but they never get out of hand.

Our conflicts can follow the same principle.

As suggested earlier, wars do not have to be atrocious or inhuman. We can change the game-rules of war to create a more humane war game. After all, wars are mind-games. If we change the rules, a new kind of drama may follow. But first, we ought to deliberately transform our perception of ourselves into that of conscious game players, and wars into games that nations play with one another.

10

Peace Dance in the Moonlight

Was there a time when there was no war? Some say it is the will of God. Some say it is God's play. It is another way of saying that wars are inevitable and nobody is responsible.

—Maharaj Shri Nisragadatta, *I Am That*

Diplomacy has rarely been able to gain at the conference table what cannot be gained or held on the battlefield.

—Gen. Walter Bedell Smith (director of the CIA, and U.S. Ambassador to Russia)

Under the influence of early-twentieth-century peace movements, President Herbert C. Hoover formulated the international Kellog-Briand Pact of 1929, renouncing wars. All major governments signed it, and the world peace movements hailed this sanctimonious event as a miracle. Historians described it, however, as show biz.

The same basic theme that marks the venues of entertainment and warfare is also found in diplomacy and peace activism. There are over one hundred and sixty peace organizations registered with the International Peace Bureau. Their members are the children of light who engage in a never-ending battle against the children of darkness. Like war, peace and diplomacy are games that nations and individuals play.

I was a player in the world peace movement during the 1980s and early 1990s, organizing peace activism first in Israel and then in the United States. My American partner was the prominent California psychologist and social activist Dale O'Neal. In Tel Aviv, my collaborator was the celebrated poet and future general-secretary of the Israeli Writers' Society, Ms. Margalit Matityahu. Both my American and Israeli colleagues were endowed with extraordinary charisma and inexhaustible physical and intellectual energy that won my admiration.

A memorable event from my peace activism period was my meeting with the Israeli Labor Party leader and future prime minister, Shimon Peres. At that time, I was also active in the Israeli Labor party. In my view, Peres has been one of the most outstanding statesmen of Israel since David Ben-Gurion, and a fervent advocate of peace between Israel ad the Arabs. I drove from Tel Aviv to meet him at the Israeli Knesset in Jerusalem, it was a hot summer day. As I waited, he stepped out of his office, dressed in a white shirt with an open collar and accompanied by another member of Parliament, and paused in front of me:

"Mr. Brenner?"

"Yes."

"I've to go to the john," he smiled; "can't hold it any longer. Do you mind joining me, and we can start our conversation on the way?"

"I don't mind," I responded instinctively.

The other Knesset member went on his way, and I walked with Peres to the members' washroom. Our discussion, which began immediately, was direct and warm. Peres was efficient, concise, extremely clear, and thoroughly informed about the intricacies of peace in the Middle East. We were way into our conversation when we reached the urinals shoulder to shoulder, and but for a brief sigh of relief our dialogue continued uninterrupted. A few short years later Peres became Israel's prime minister, and I was seeking inner peace, meditating with Zen monks on Mount Baldi in California.

Peace Dance in the Moonlight

During those years, I was inspired by the belief that I could convince the Israeli society about the merits of peaceful coexistence with their Arab neighbors. After a long period of intense activity that wore me out, I faded from the world reconciliation scene with growing earnestness to find my own inner tranquillity. Meanwhile, Prime Minister Yitzhak Rabin was assassinated. As of the time of this writing there was still no peace in the Middle East.

People love to pray for peace in public, to deliver exhilarating speeches in action-packed rallies, or to get arrested and make newspaper headlines. It is a game filled with idealism, passion, and rhetoric, always in labor, rarely giving birth.

Yes, world peace is an exciting theatre. When the terrorist Yassir Arafat, head of the PLO, spoke to the UN General Assembly in New York, he wore two pistols hanging from his waist like a character out of *Lawrence of Arabia*. The humor grew when he was later awarded the Nobel Prize for *peace*. Unfortunately, the Israelis did not learn from this event to treat problematic situations with irony.

And yet, life's events are filled with irony. After Prime Minister Menachem Begin and President Anwar Sadat received their joint Nobel Prize for peace, Begin started the infamous war in Lebanon that lasted three years, and Sadat was assassinated. It is ironic that prominent leaders of the world peace movement, such as Mahatma Gandhi, Martin Luther King Jr., Sadat, and Yitzhak Rabin have suffered violent deaths at the hands of their own people. Perhaps the time has come that we, as a society and as its leaders and individual members, develop a more playful attitude toward everything that we do.

In his gentle poem "The Plight of Man," Ron J. Flemming writes:

> I've seen an eagle in effortless flight
> I've seen the stars shining in the night
> I've watched men struggle, and seen them fight
> While they say they're walking in the light . . .
> Days begin; then centuries pass
> Sand trickles down this solar hourglass
> Life moves ahead, it is here then gone
> Not a matter of right or wrong. . . .[1]

Alexander's Ideal: A World United in Peace

Without peaceful people how can you have peace in the world? As long as people are as they are, the world must be as it is.

—Nisragadatta, *I Am That*

The noble ideology of the Macedonian hero, Alexander the Great, was to unite the ancient world in harmonious existence. To fulfill his passion, inspired by his renowned tutor the Greek philosopher Aristotle, Alexander spend his entire reign on battlefields, conquering the Persian Empire, India, and Egypt. One year after his father, King Philip II, was murdered, twenty-one-year-old Alexander began his famous unifying crusades, which kept him away from home and denied him peace and joy for the rest of his life.

Alexander managed to overcome a large part of the ancient world, but he failed to establish world peace or unity. To drown his disillusionment, he drank. For fear of falling asleep, lest someone would murder him, he read philosophy throughout the nights, keeping his dagger close under his pillow. Upon contracting a raging fever, after the alcohol weakened his immune system, he died in his tent at the age of thirty-three.

As Robert E. Neale has insightfully commented, individuals who are burdened with inner conflict cannot stand outer discord,[2] and are often overcome by it.

The Game of a City of Happy People

To him that has no peace in his heart, there is no place to build the Holy Temple. For how can the carpenter build in the midst of a whirlwind? From the parched clay can grow no living thing.

—*The Gospel of the Essenes*

The Essenes, known in today's world as the authors of the Dead Sea Scrolls, were a Hebrew sect that lived in a segregated community by the Dead Sea in the Israeli desert. One of the things less known about them is that they played an intriguing game called the "Sevenfold Peace." Every day they lit a candle, and seven candles on Saturday, to remind them of the peace they pursued each day in another area of life.

The sevenfold peace consisted of peace with the body; peace with the mind; peace with the family; peace with humanity (neighbors, coworkers, and community members); peace with the culture (the surrounding traditions, religions, and worldviews); peace with the environment; and peace with their God.

This game, according to Dio Chrysostom and Josephus Plavius, contributed to the Essenes being "a whole city of happy people."[3]

Conversely, Kathy and Larry have been married for sixteen years, when Kathy met Stuart on the Internet. After corresponding with Stuart by e-mail for about a year, she asked her husband for a divorce. Kathy was a journalist, but she stopped working when Joyce, then fourteen years old, was born. Larry has a Ph.D. in computer science and works for Microsoft. Without mentioning Stuart, Kathy told her husband:

"I need space, Larry; I want a divorce as soon as possible."

"Without warning, after sixteen years of marriage?"

"You should have known it was coming, Larry. You should have recognized my hints," she told him.

Kathy and fourteen-year-old Joyce moved into an apartment a few blocks away from the house, and Joyce stopped talking to her father. Kathy also became active in a local Californian peace group. Her new friends on the Internet and at the peace group supported and coached her dogfight with Larry for child support and alimony, and she sued for a significant portion of their assets:

"You owe me," she rationalized with Larry. "I gave you sixteen years of my life, and a daughter who loves you."

His pleas with both Kathy and Joyce were of no avail. After ten months, and $10,500 in attorney fees, supplied by Kathy's father, Kathy and Larry were divorced. She started to go out with Stuart openly, and a few weeks later she dropped out of the peace movement.

Indeed, with Neale echoing the literary moralist François De La Rochefoucauld, it is frivolous to earnestly seek peace for others when one is unable to find it within oneself.

Sixty-five-year-old Mary Ann came out of the supermarket carrying large grocery bags. The sun simmered mercilessly; the temperature was 106 degrees. She was anxious to get home and store the dairy products in the refrigerator. As she approached her car, she found the way to her car door blocked by a shopping cart, left behind by another shopper. At that moment, the van next to her began to pull out:

"Why are you looking at me like that?" bawled the young woman through the rolled window, as she drove the van away.

Frustrated and puffing, the old woman placed her bags on the parking lot baking asphalt, then, perspiring and wheezing, dragged the young woman's cart out of the way so that she would be able to unlock her car.

Life cannot be fun, if we murder our own and each other's joy of living. Sometimes we abandon our shopping cart in the parking lot in other people's way. Sometimes we let the cart roll into someone's parked car. Sometimes we carelessly back our truck into someone else's vehicle, causing other people a financial loss. These actions are acts of violence.

Dan and Virginia-Beth rented our house on the pacific coast for nearly two years. After they vacated, our well pump and other items were missing, along with some damage that was done to the house and needed repair. We used the well to irrigate the yard. We decided to deduct $112 from their security deposit.

A few days later we received a nasty letter from them, drafted by an attorney, accusing us of withholding the clients' security deposit "unlawfully, without proof or good reason." It was a declaration of war. Our options were either to go to a small claims court, or to forgo the debt.

After deliberation, my wife and I decided that our time and stress were not worth it, although both law and justice were on our side. To make a point, however, we mailed them a check for $124, 10 percent over the disputed amount. We figured it would get their attention and spur their conscience. Two months later, Dan and Virginia-Beth knocked on our door unexpectedly, holding a basket of fresh vegetables from their new garden, and the missing pump that they "happened to find" as they unpacked the boxes.

The Inside of a Cup

Cleanse the inside of the cup and of the plate, that the outside also may be clean.

—Matt. 23:26

Whenever we practice racial, religious, or age discrimination; whenever we participate in a conspiracy to cheat another; whenever we compete to deliberately ruin another person's livelihood; whenever we advertise with the intention to rob someone's retirement nest egg; whenever we exploit someone's handicap, misfortune, or vulnerability in order to make a profit; whenever we abuse, intimidate, or rudely insult someone to destroy their self-respect and human dignity, knowingly or unknowingly we use deadly firearms and therefore engage in war. No rationale or ideology can change that. Numerous anecdotes have been woven to illustrate the violent nature of many of our everyday acts, violence we take for granted alongside our ideological rhetoric about world peace and Tikun Olam (world fixing).

There are various forms of violence, both criminal and non-criminal. Their legal distinction merely describes gradations of a single phenomenon. The question we ought perhaps to ask ourselves is—can a universal ideal be attained in a society whose members neglect it at the personal level?

Gandhi did not believe that, writing: "If one does not practice non-violence in one's personal relations with others and hopes to use it in bigger affairs, one is vastly mistaken."[4] Assuming that Ghandi, De La Rochefoucauld, and Neale were correct, then a philanthropist who makes large financial contributions to support the human rights movement, but who abuses employees or members of his own family, will not remove human rights abuse from the world.

When Patricia ended a three-year term on the board of her church, she wanted to stay on for another year. Being generous with both her time and money, she received recognition and respect from her community and no one uttered a syllable when she quietly remained on the board, although it was against church bylaws. Members could only serve one year, with an option to stay a second year, but after two years they had to step down.

When Patricia announced that she was staying on for a fourth year, a board member finally raised the legal question:

"I served the first of a two-year term," Patricia replied, referring only to her last year on the board. "I'm entitled to stay on for another year."

"But you've already served a year over the maximum time allotted in the bylaws," Joe, the new board member, contested. "If you insist on continuing, we must call a community meeting and vote to change the bylaws."

Unprepared for such firm resistance to her otherwise unchallenged authority, Patricia stood up and loudly accused Joe of intimidating her, crying:

"This *terrible man* frightens me. I refuse to serve on the board with such an evil man!" Announcing her resignation, Patricia stormed out of the meeting.

I realize that there is a great deal of anger in our society, and I hope everyone sees that. It is brewing in women, men, and teenagers. That is why we have the highest violence and teenage crime ratios in the entire industrial world. Here, again, treating life as a game can take on a special meaning because it can neutralize some of our anger, frustration, and impatience.

In a capitalistic economy that also emphasizes individualism, the individual is extremely vulnerable. Hence, it would be meritorious to be able to take ourselves more lightly, and remember that we are role- and game-players.

Having said that, I also recognize the fact that the undertaking of this sociopsychological challenge would be enhanced if such an attitude were considered politically correct, culturally accepted, and pursued by public opinion leaders and academia. The challenge of adopting a playful attitude toward existence would become less of a feat if it enjoyed widespread support rather than being attempted sporadically in isolated contexts. In order to carry on as members of society, individuals need the permission of their society to change the rules of the game.

In the next chapter we will peruse the important scientific studies and leading theories pertaining to the adoption of a playful attitude toward life, the psychological benefits derived from applying it to everyday situations, and the healing qualities attributed to conscious game- and role-play in therapy.

11

Theories of Play and Healing

Reviewing Research

Play has an almost unlimited number of aspects. The better-known theories of play have been criticized not so much because of their lack of validity but because of their incompleteness. The whole truth regarding play cannot be known until the whole truth regarding life itself is known.

—Harvey C. Lehman and Paul A. Witty,
The Psychology of Play Activities

Scientists began to research the psychological, physiological, and social gain derived from play at the turn of the nineteenth century. The classical theories of the German scholar Friedrich von Schiller and the English philosopher Herbert Spencer are the most frequently cited by many American scholars who have studied the applications and benefits of a playful attitude.

Michael J. Ellis was a research professor at the University of Illinois, and director of a play research laboratory funded by the American National Institute of Mental Health. In his book *Why*

People Play, now a classic, he lists five classical and five contemporary theories about play. They represent the modern evolution of our understanding of the human instinct to be playful.

Five Classical Theories of Play

Play, along with the basic needs of nutrition, health, shelter and education, is vital for the development of the potential of all children.

—The Malta Declaration of the International Association for the Child's Right to Play

I will not dwell on the classical theories. I will only mention them here briefly in order to provide a historical perspective and a philosophical framework for the contemporary precepts discussed in the next section. The five classical theories stipulate the following:

a. that our will to play is fundamentally a need to discharge surplus energy;
b. that play is a natural compulsion because it relaxes us;
c. that play is instinctive, with no particular aim;
d. that play is an inherent instinct to teach and learn, and to prepare our youths for adult life; a similar play instinct is inborn in all living species;
e. that what we call "play" is an unconscious desire to recapitulate the evolutionary development of our species, and that this instinct is prevalent in all species.

Theory	*Benefit Highlights*
Surplus energy	Discharges surplus of energy; necessary for psychological and physiological survival
Relaxation	Allows recuperation from stress; necessary to emit responses other than those typically used at work
Instinct	An inherited, unlearned capacity to act playfully for its own sake and for no particular known or recognized aim
Preparation	An inherited instinct to exert an effort in preparation for a later part of life

| Recapitulation | An inherited instinct to recapitulate the history of the development of the particular species in the individual organism's own development |

In critiquing the classical theories, Ellis explains that because play, and the need to play, exist, classical theorists assumed that it exists in order to fulfill utilitarian functions relating to survival. The classical theories focus on children, and do not explain the adults' intense interest in toys that utilize modern technology, such as sailing, car racing, gliding, dirt bikes, slot machines, and stuffed animals. These cannot be instinctive means for survival.

Ellis contends that our children are playful because it is an *instinctive* and a *natural* need. Children neither play to recuperate from work, nor to learn how to behave, how to carry out duties, or how to survive as adults. Children play because it is intrinsic to human nature. Likewise, he has noticed that the very animals that play most are also the animals that exhibit variable and adaptive behavior.[1]

J. C. Friedrich von Schiller

Man has two basic needs: the need to discharge energy, and the need to design experience.

—J. C. Friedrich von Schiller

Perhaps the most influential classical play theorist was J. C. Friedrich von Schiller, a German philosopher, historian, and poet. He saw the human being as motivated by two basic instincts, the need to be serious and the need to be playful. They can function either simultaneously and in harmony, or in conflict with each other. When they are in harmony, a person feels complete, free, and creative. Conflicts are common because one need usually ignores or overrides the other. Much of what we experience, according to Schiller, are our back-and-forth attempts to satisfy both needs, for instance, discharge of energy brings pleasure, and the need for meaning brings a sense of security. But a temporary exercise of either of them brings only a limited satisfaction, spoiled by lack of the other.[2]

Thus, Neale expounds: "the person who sees oneself consistently as one who is at play in the world, is expressing one's state of inner-harmony."[3]

Five Contemporary Theories of Play

In April of 1975, psychologists, sociologists, anthropologists, and educators from all over the United States gathered in Detroit to discuss current research about the ramifications of play. At the end of that conference, they decided to make it the first annual meeting of the American Association for the Anthropological Study of Play, and to continue a collaborative investigation of the subject.

According to Ellis, five contemporary theories developed in the United States during the twentieth century:

a. Play is the emotional need to repeat rewarding experiences.
b. Playfulness satisfies psychic needs that do not get fulfilled otherwise. It provides an outlet for pleasant experiences that we cannot obtain in other activities including work.
c. A playful attitude allows us to control and redirect aggression, frustration and hostility, while it reduces both emotional and physiological tension. Hence, it serves as catharsis. However, if we encourage aggression in any way, even in a playful way, it only increases hostility rather than reducing it. The very planning of activities to provide outlets for fighting or competitive purposes sanctions aggression.
d. Play is therapeutic, and leads to psychological healing. By repeating playfully unpleasant experiences, we reduce their hold over us and allow their assimilation.
e. Play is an effective tool for learning, investigating, exploring, taking apart, and re-creating elements of our surroundings. Thus, it enhances our ability to adapt to and control our environment.[4]

Professor Brian Sutton-Smith is considered to have great influence on modern psychologists, anthropologists, historians, communication experts, educators, sports sociologists, and sports-medicine experts who work with, study, or research the efficacy of play. He stated what presently seems to be a consensus in the field, that a playful spirit contributes to well-being, and is often characteristic of mentally, emotionally, physically, and socially healthier individuals.[5]

Pleasure versus Utility

Society benefits from the overall climate that playfulness of its members creates. It breeds respect for people as people, and not as representatives of specific socioeconomic strata.

—Cor Westland and Jane Knight, *Playing, Living, Learning*

A prevalent misconception among scientists is that play is not utilitarian, that it is for pleasure and self-satisfaction alone. In their perception, as soon as anything becomes utilitarian, it becomes work and ceases to be play. To them, only when a child catches imaginary balloons, pretends to be a cat, or makes believe that a doll is a baby, it is play. But when the child washes a doll's real clothes with real water and real soap, it is work. When the child arranges balloons in a party, or when an adult does it in inaugurations and nomination conventions, it is work. Likewise, it can no longer be considered play to these scientists when an adult plays the role of doctor, teacher, or member of the House of Representatives, because it is utilitarian.

As a social psychologist Susanna Millar has pointed out, mothers, fathers, grannies, uncles, aunts, older brothers and sisters, teachers, and neighbors teach the child to be utilitarian, and reward the child for repeating utilitarian acts. We do the same thing with our pets. Thus, gradually, the child learns to play "seriously" rather than spontaneously and for sheer joy—for the child's acceptance by society, not for the child's pleasure.[6]

In this process, we deprive ourselves of a natural and ongoing mental rejuvenation, forced to constantly operate on the brink of emotional exhaustion. Dr. Millar demonstrates this assertion in the case of the child who is tired from a long walk, but perks up and trots home rapidly at the mere suggestion of being able to play upon arrival, and the baby who, although badly in need of sleep and rest, instinctively yells for toys. Even a dog that is tired from a trip, or recuperating after surgery, charges out at the opportunity to play.

Prof. Lewis Terman and the Famous "Termites"

When Lewis Terman was head of the psychology department at Stanford University, he began his celebrated, long-term, and exhaustive survey of gifted children with IQs of 140 to 200. He watched and monitored their lives for forty years. He recorded the history of their health, personality, intellectual achievements, interests, and the types of games they played. Over the years, Terman's subjects became known as the "termites." The data that was collected on them, was compared to another group of participants—of the same age but with lower IQ scores, mostly of average intelligence.

The members of the gifted group consistently preferred mental games and demonstrated less interest in competitive games. However, their physical and mental health, stability, and social adjustment were significantly and consistently above the members of the other group.

These conclusions were supported by other empirical findings. According to Millar, various studies conducted with children have also confirmed that higher-functioning children tend to be more versatile, resourceful, mature, and *more playful* than their average contemporaries.[7]

Hence, these scientists suggest, a possible link has been found to exist between playfulness and intellectual flexibility, enhanced ability to grasp new things, and a resourceful functioning in society.

Play Therapy and Healing

Play is a therapy, and now that this fact is better recognized, the number of patients in need of it is far greater. But more than that, it has a prophylactic value.

—Karl Menninger

Freud's contribution to this field of research began with his observation that while children want to be grown-ups, grown-ups want to be children. After developing hypnosis as a vehicle for psychoanalysis to treat mental illness, Freud replaced it with free association talk. Many Freudian analysts continue to use free play along with verbal free association to help patients overcome inhibitions and anxieties.

Today there are a number of healing modalities that utilize the concept of play therapy. Role-play in particular is for many of us still mostly unconscious. Thus, bringing it to the forefront of patients' awareness in therapy has emerged as a means for healing.

Robert J. Landy, a drama therapist, describes in his informative book *Persona and Performance*, which also makes for entertaining reading due to his lively writing style, numerous cases of healing through the utilization of role-play. The following is his report of Michael:

Michael is a twenty-seven-year-old gay man, from an upper middle-class family. He is highly verbal, intelligent, and analytical. He came to Dr. Landy because of an intense fear of AIDS and bugs, a number of psychosomatic illnesses, and an unbearable sense of isolation and loneliness. Michael's sexual relationships left him with a feeling of being used and emptiness. In his mind, he was a victim. As a young boy, he felt victimized by his father, a successful businessman, who used to walk around the house naked and do push-ups also naked. During role play therapy, Michael preferred the role of a naive child who communed with nature and who avoided the evil ways of grown-ups. Conscious role play gave Michael the awareness of the role he played unconsciously since an early age, and he was able to move on with his life and change his helpless act to that of helping others; ultimately he went to law school.[8]

In Landy's experience, conscious role-play allows an individual to simultaneously "be *and* not to be." Being in role, and at the same time being "de-roled," means that a person is able to observe and reflect upon one's own act. In other words, conscious role-play allows us to act reflectively.[9]

Another dramatic illustration of healing through play, provided by Landy, is the case of thirty-year-old Ann, the daughter of an alcoholic father. Since the tender age of nine, Ann felt compelled to "rescue" her father from his murderous feelings toward himself, just like the rescuers in the game alcoholics play. As she grew up, she conceived her life's role to be that of a martyr, the one to sacrifice herself so that the rest of her family would "survive" by maintaining their psychological integrity. Since she left home, she lived in fifteen houses, but none of them felt safe to her. Every time she moved, she hoped it would be a new beginning.

In drama therapy, Ann's everyday role as a martyr became suddenly clear to her. She could see how and why she had consistently denied her own needs, in order to "protect" the needs of the other members of her family. Once she became aware of the role she played in the outer world, she could take on another role by which she would live her own life.[10]

In their critical book, *Arenas of the Mind,* Lillian Back and Merla Wolk cite the following excerpt, written by Jennie, a young student. In it, Jennie refers to all her roles in the outer world as "masks":

> Okay, I wear a mask. I know I do. It's a personality mask. All my friends and acquaintances think I'm always happy and smiling; I never show any anger. I'm never mad in front of people or express any anger over personal conflicts with my friends. I'm considered the nicest person among my friends.
>
> Well, this "nicest" person is a monster at home. That's where I take all my anger and frustration out, and my family suffers for it. For a long time the entire family was scared of me, and I'm sure my two darling sisters hated me. Every family member was puzzled at the number of friends I have; they did not understand how a monster like me could get along with anybody on the face of the earth.[11]

We can see that Jennie is playing in public the role of the "perfect woman," although she is ambivalent about it, whereas, the role she is playing within her family has made her feel miserable. That's because although she abuses them, Jennie loves her parents and sisters. She even calls her sisters "darlings."

According to Landy, now that Jennie has become conscious of her roles, she is freer to step back, explore her games with other people with detachment, and give up the ones that make her unhappy for another type of role that would make her happier.

Role-Play and Creativity

One of the pivotal concepts in relation to play is that it is spontaneous.
—Adam and Allee Blatner, *The Art of Play*

It is a recurring theme among modern play researchers, that conscious role-and-game play transforms existence into an adventure. When we act consciously, we can take chances, explore, and experiment in all areas of our everyday lives. As role-players we can look at the world and judge our experiences with a more relaxed, creative, and effective view.

That and more. Some scholars assert that the sheer fact that we all actually love to play, indicates an inherently deep need that is beyond recreation, and that is the need for free self-expression. It underlies our desire to *make* our roles, rather than merely to *take* them and act them out unconsciously. What we really want is to be able to shape them. Therefore it is not surprising that the founder of psychodrama, J. L. Moreno, was a psychiatrist from Vienna whose passion was theater. His genius was in conceiving that people can actually become role-players rather than remain as role-takers.

The Perils of Illusion in Play

The art of living is the art of knowing how to believe lies.

—Cesare Pavese (Italian author)

Since the word *illusion* has a specific connotation in our language, I wish to distinguish it from my references in this book to *conscious role-play* and *playful spirit*. The reason I bring this up is that in Latin, *illudere* means "to play," or "to be in play," including the acts of deliberate pretense and make-believe. In English, the term *illusion* often suggests doing tricks or creating a deceptive or misleading impression of reality. By contrast, acting consciously—rather than doing something automatically—is anything but deception, unless it is intended to be so. A conscious actor, even while being totally absorbed in one's role and game, does not normally mistake "appearance" for "reality." A child, who stands on a heap of boxes and sways his arms, normally knows he or she is not a pilot, nor an airplane.[12]

I propose, although I did not find scientific proof for it, that our need to deceive ourselves, and others, will decline as we become increasingly conscious actors.

Animals at Play

Joy often expresses itself in play, which many animals indulge in all their lives. Biologists continue to be dismayed by the lay public's interest in possible links between animal play and human creativity.

—Jeffrey Moussaieff Masson and Susan McCarthy,
When Elephants Weep

When my dog Casey is uncomfortable during play, he growls. When the game is adequately suitable to his temperament, his mouth becomes enveloped with a smile, his eyes sparkle, and he makes frequent sounds of joy.

Some zoologists believe that play is characteristic of, and richer among, the higher-evolved animals.[13] They maintain that there is a link between an animal's ability to learn and its playfulness.

Animals vary to the extent that they explore their environment either for fun or out of curiosity, in accordance with their level of intelligence and degree of complexity. Most mammals, for instance, spend a great deal of time exploring, investigating, and manipulating objects, out of inquisitiveness.

There is ample empirical evidence in the literature to suggest that intelligent animals at play are aware that they pretend. From my personal experience, I believe that is true with dogs. Casey, our male Keeshound, invites me to fun-fight almost every evening. He stretches his body and barks at me enticingly, or he pulls at the hem of my pants. When my wife and I play with him, we are comfortable placing our hand between his jaws knowing he would never bite it. When he jumps toward us, he bounces like a large gentle cat, hardly jostling us in spite of his fifty pounds and enormous strength. Yet, when he is angry or threatened by strangers, he may turn vicious. An intelligent dog discriminates expertly between playful and hostile situations.

Particularly illustrative are the decorous demonstrations of dignity characteristic of certain dogs, and I understand that is true also of certain wolves. Keeshounds, for instance, walk with a stately manner and imposing gait, holding their tail erect, consciously expressing their self-respect and perceived social standing in the animal kingdom. We had a female Keeshound, Yamit, who walked in the street with such a self-aware manner—a proudly erect tail and wiggling hips—that it drew the attention of most passersby. She enjoyed the fascination she deliberately generated, thoroughly and profoundly, though we never taught her to do that.

In the course of my research, I have learned that birds, dolphins, and whales are notoriously playful. Ibis perform flight acrobatics, individually and collectively. They swoop, twist, and turn. Eider ducks repeatedly dive through swirling waters and launch themselves on streaming rapids.[14] Dolphins and whales play chasing one another. They throw dead fish into the air like balls and catch them without eating them. Young dolphins repeatedly catch small fish and then let them go; they turn somersaults outside the water; they bring up stones from the bottom of the ocean to spit at onlookers, and they play with floating objects.[15]

Chimpanzees enact a great variety of acrobatic games: they climb, slide, jump, turn in the air, and carry bricks on their backs, all in a playful manner. They look at the world inquisitively upside down through their legs; they punch a hole through a leaf and peer through it; they contemplate their reflection in a puddle of water and utter cries of joy. They march together in a circle, to the banging rhythm of old tins.[16] Monkeys play practical jokes on each other. And happy gorillas sing.

Elephants dislodge and roll dry clay, and are particularly frisky. And lions, both young and adults, carry on a gentle melodrama, rub cheeks, and lick each other.[17] Chickens' pecking order is secured through show-fight. Once the social hierarchy is established, it remains fixed until the next arrival of hens. Injuries are rare and accidental, as is the case with many fun-fighting animals. Most animals may kill other species for food, but not for fun, nor out of malice, and not their own species.

After conducting her own research, Millar has concluded that play for animals is as natural as searching for food, shelter, and mates.[18]

According to Masson and McCarthy, our domestication of animals reduces their desire for play. That is so, because, in captivity, animals experience little joy in life. A change in their natural environment often terrifies them, causing their happiness and general activity, including play, to deteriorate. Conversely, improved conditions over time may revive their will to play. In their stirring book, *When Elephants Weep,* Masson and McCarthy write: "That a tiger is condemned to a slow death by boredom unless it finds pleasure in performing [for humans], is a sad commentary on what humans have done to these magnificent predators."[19]

One of the questions that puzzles researchers is: Why do youngsters play more than adult animals? The answer is that they do not. What has happened here, too, is that human researchers tend to perceive play only when it is not utilitarian. When an external stimuli enables scientists to explain an activity functionally, they tend to treat it no longer as play.

Like humans, when animals are deprived of food, they search for it. When it is abundant, they play with it. As Masson and McCarthy have correctly asserted: "The grim tasks of survival, even surviving well, do not make a lot of people happy."[20] Animals exhibit such pure joy even while they engage in mundane and routine functional activities. Why can't we?

12

Life Is Tough, Tough But Fun

To take life seriously and yet to be able to play; and while playing ever to keep a serious corner in one's mind. To keep an open heart for the things of this world and never to fly from the world through contempt for them, knowing that they must not be taken too seriously.

—Socrates

Hugo Rahner, a historian of religion, reminds us that the Greeks knew the value of the spirit of play much better than we do today. Although Socrates jested, he meant it, said Xenophon about the master.

The obstacles to happiness in our own era are complex and numerous. We are embroiled in predicaments that stem from our traditional ways of approaching life, society, and emotional survival. Consequently, we feel sorry for ourselves for not having the things we fancy—a certain car, house, or job; we experience anguish because we were born into a particular socioeconomic setting, or because we were not born into other specific economic or political circumstances. These things make us suffer; they may make us feel miserable; they may make us feel unhappy. But we almost always feel good about ourselves when we are aware of the fact that we play a role well, even when the situation itself is less than desirable, or when the outcome we had hoped for has not unfolded. Joy does not mean having no strain and no pain.

The essence of every game is adventure. Adventures do not have to be sugarcoated. In approaching our daily pursuits and life's events gamefully, we can find happiness at the heart of being.

Early at dawn, I walk three to four miles on most days, winter and summer. I am often alone then. Walking briskly during a storm into a brute wet wind that slashes against my cheeks, I sometimes sing: "The weather is rough, but I am tough. Life is harsh, harsh but fun." Sitting in my car at traffic lights, I sometimes count to find out how long it lasts for the system to change from red to green. It usually takes ten to fifteen seconds. These are some of the little games I play with myself throughout the day.

Laughter heals and uplifts even when we laugh alone. Once my wife fell ill. She lay fatigued in bed, and for lack of energy to do anything else she contemplated life. She was overtaken by a seizure of laughter that lasted quite awhile. After that, she felt better. Later she told me:

"At the height of my distress I looked out the window and saw a smiling cloud. God was reminding me to laugh."

A conscious player can be at once both serious and playful: "Those who have observed children at play have no doubt about their seriousness,"[1] wrote Robert E. Neale. Unfortunately, he added, "fun" is still one of the most abused concepts in our culture. Modern "funsters" seek to escape life rather than to engage in it.

With our cultural focus on utilitarianism and earnestness, the existing play research pertains to either its educational and training aspects, or its entertainment and recreation context. I believe that it is time now to direct interdisciplinary attention to the efficacy of adopting a general playful attitude toward life and in developing it as a societal norm.

The reality is that we are all masterful role-players. All of us can act as "a passionate faithful lover one minute, a libertine the next, and a platonic ideologist a day later,"[2] using Anna Nardo's poetic line. That is also what Henri Bergson, a French philosopher and Nobel laureate, meant when he said that our lives are a theater of unending creation.

As we saw in the previous chapter, some scientists stress the link between a spirit of play, the ability to grasp new things, and our intellectual flexibility as well as creativity. Conscious role-play frees us to experiment with our ideas and emotions openly and without self-blame, to dare, to make mistakes and fail and not to feel guilty about it.

We can learn to accept situational constraints without feeling stuck or victimized once we choose a role within those boundaries that we can enjoy playing. I hope that this work has made it clear that we are not locked into the roles we find ourselves playing. Two courses of action are available to everyone of us. We can remain in the game but take on a new role that is more enjoyable than the present one. Or we can switch into a completely new game and a new role.

Theoretically, our democratic society and liberal culture allow us to do these things. However, the stern emphases on competitiveness, winning, and taking everything so damn seriously restrict the range of psychological exploration that is available to us. Only conscious and courageous role-play enables us to express our souls more freely.

Indeed, a general playful disposition toward our very existence belongs in the domain of one's *emotional survival*. It can become a new meaning for our lives as individuals in an increasingly complex society. By treating life as an endless series of games, we set ourselves free from the claws of bare existence, thus liberating ourselves from a destiny of mere survival.

Spirited individuals are often more popular, more sought out, and make better companions. As various scientific studies reveal, frisky and creative individuals are more likely to be chosen as leaders. Young children who are imaginative and playful have been found to be able to sit patiently for much longer periods, without getting destructively restless, than children of the same age and intelligence whose playful tendencies are more suppressed.[3]

Why is it, asks Hugo Rahner, that "the child, the supreme and most obvious example of man at play, has been made the very symbol and personification of that life of blessedness, which we have lost and which we so ardently yearn to regain? Why is it that in every civilization, religious men have symbolized the nature of life in the world to come as a wonderfully carefree and supremely happy dance?"[4]

You and I have come a long way from the first chapter of this book. Remember the title—*If Life Is a Game, How Come I'm Not Having Fun?* Fun, we have seen, may be inherent in most of our activities and pursuits, as long as they are approached as adventures. An attitude, unlike an activity, is mental. It takes place in our inner worlds, and therefore is unobservable. Only the player knows about it; the rest of us intuit it. The idea is to reclaim the fun inherent in our actions, which we have neglected as a result of developing the attitude we currently have toward life.

Perhaps no other image better concludes our pilgrimage to playfulness than the one offered by David L. Miller:

> Anthropologists study ancient societies in terms of their urge to play.
> Sociologists study human interactions as social games with definite rules.
> Psychologists find the meaning of life in our games and ploys.
> To communication theorists, the media is a game.
> Theologians play with the most sacred religious rituals.
> Philosophers play with ideas, knowing that they constitute our experiences.
> Mathematicians play with decisions as if they are game theories.
> To universities, academic discourses are games scholars play.
> Writers and historians play with words.
> "Play is the thing."[5]

As Michel de Montaigne expressed it:

We can be like children who spend a day, every day, in a park—"a park filled with many gardens and playgrounds and azure-tinted lakes with white boats sailing upon the tranquil waves."[6]

Epilogue

For certain fortunate people there is something which transcends all classifications of behavior, and that is awareness; and something that rises above the programming of the past, and that is spontaneity; and something that is more rewarding than games, and that is intimacy.

—Eric Berne, Games People Play

It has been a long journey. And I thank you for your steady perseverance. We are ensnared in dilemmas that are steeped in our conventional approach to our existence, including how we perceive role-play in our enigmatic societal structure. The idea that our lives can be treated as a series of games we play with each other has brought to the foreground a confrontation with contemporary philosophical assertions and the definitions we have attributed to such fundamental issues as work, happiness, success, war, peace, religion, freedom of will, role-enactment, play, and a spirit of play.

I hope that my humble attempt to bring to light an overlooked aspect of ourselves as individuals who think, feel, function, and interact within the confines of a society that plays games in order to operate, has been fruitful. Although we dwell in private inner worlds, we act and find meaning and happiness in the outer world. That outer world is the civilized amphitheater where we put on garb and create the games and roles that constitute the experience of our lives.

Recognizing that we are a "Playing Species"—Homo Ludens—may be instrumental to finding happiness and joy in life's game. For, as Hugo Rahner's illuminated words convey:

> The same things that give human play its unique character—the light-hearted relaxing of the mind, the charm of a certain smiling contempt for mundane things, the wisdom of ease and detachment—also make it possible for a person to kick the world away from oneself with the airy grace of a dancer, and yet, at the same time, press it to one's heart.[1]

Notes

Introduction

1. Thomas Hobbes, *Leviathan*, ed. C. B. MacPherson (London: Penguin Books, 1991).
2. Allen V. Sapora and Elmer D. Mitchell, *The Theory of Play and Recreation*, 3rd ed. (New York: Ronald Press, 1961), 72.
3. Susanna Millar, *The Psychology of Play* (Baltimore: Penguin Books, 1968), 20.

Chapter 1: What Life Is in the Modern Era

1. Robert E. Neale, *In Praise of Play: Toward a Psychology of Religion* (New York: Harper & Row, 1969), 175; Harvey C. Lehman and Paul A. Witty, *The Psychology of Play Activities* (New York: A. S. Barnes, 1927; reprint, New York: Arno Press, 1976), 1 (page citations are to the reprint edition).
2. Adam Blatner, M.D. and Allee Blatner, *The Art of Play: An Adult's Guide to Reclaiming Imagination and Spontaneity* (New York: Human Sciences Press, 1988), 28.
3. Karl Jaspers, *The Great Philosophers*, vol. 2 (Orlando, FL: Harcourt Brace, 1966), 82.
4. Plotinus, *The Enneads*, part 3, 2:15, in *Great Books of the Western World*, vol. 17, trans. Stephen McKenna and B. S. Page (Chicago: Encyclopaedia Britannica, 1952).
5. Luther Halsey Gulick, M.D., *A Philosophy of Play* (Washington, DC: McGrath Publishing, 1920), 267.
6. Peter L. Berger, *The Precarious Vision: A Sociologist Looks at Social Fictions and Christian Faith* (New York: Doubleday, 1961), 67.

7. *Curry Coastal Pilot*, 6 May 1998, sec. 1B; 27 May 1998, sec. 1B.

8. Robert J. Landy, *Persona and Performance: The Meaning of Role in Drama, Therapy, and Everyday Life* (New York: Guilford Press, 1993), 18.

9. Frank Salamone, "Religion as Play," in *The Anthropological Study of Play: Problems and Prospects, Proceedings of the First Annual Meeting of the Association for the Anthropological Study of Play*, eds. David F. Lancy and B. Allan Tindall (Cornwall, NY: Leisure Press, 1976), 155.

10. Anne Lamott, *bird by bird* (New York: Doubleday, 1994), 3.

11. Johan Huizinga, *Homo Ludens: A Study of the Play Element in Culture* (Boston: Beacon Press, 1955), quoted in *Motivations in Play, Games, and Sports*, eds. Ralph Slovenko and James A. Knight (Springfield, IL: Charles C. Thomas Publishing, 1967), foreword, xxvii.

Chapter 2: The Parallel Worlds We Live In

1. David L. Miller, *Gods and Games: Toward a Theology of Play* (New York: Harper Colophon Books, 1973), 138.

2. Robert E. Neale, *In Praise of Play: Toward a Psychology of Religion* (New York: Harper & Row, 1969), 26.

3. Will Durant, *The Story of Civilization, Part II* (New York: Simon & Schuster, 1975), 242.

4. Julian Jaynes, *The Origin of Consciousness in the Breakdown of the Bicameral Mind* (Boston: Houghton, 1976), 1.

5. Rodney Stark and William Sims Bainbridge, *The Future of Religion: Secularization, Revival, and Cult Formation* (Berkeley: University of California Press, 1985), 2.

6. "Adam Smith," *The Money Game* (New York: Random House, 1967), 11.

7. Frank E. Manning, "The Rediscovery of Religious Play: A Pentecostal Case," in *The Anthropological Study of Play: Problems and Prospects, Proceedings of the First Annual Meeting of the Association for the Anthropological Study of Play*, eds. David F. Lancy and B. Allan Tindall (Cornwall, NY: Leisure Press, 1976), 140–144.

8. Neale, *In Praise of Play*, 92.

9. Frank Salamone, "Religion as Play," in *Anthropological Study of Play*, Lancy and Tindall, 147–155.

10. Stark and Bainbridge, *The Future of Religion*, 10–11.

11. Neale, "Play and the Sacred," in *Motivations in Play, Games and Sports*, eds. Ralph Slovenko and James A. Knight (Springfield, IL: Charles C. Thomas Publishing, 1967), 154–155.

12. Neale, *In Praise of Play*, 98–99.

13. Stark and Bainbridge, *Future of Religion*, 5.

14. Roger Caillois, "Play and the Sacred," quoted in *In Praise of Play*, Neale, 95.

15. T. J. Scheff, *Catharsis in Healing, Ritual, and Drama* (Berkeley: University of California Press, 1979), 115, 148.

16. Lisa Beyer, "Crazy? Hey, You Never Know," *Time*, 17 April 1995, 22.

17. Neale, *In Praise of Play*, 152–153.

Chapter 3: Persona and Performance

1. Stephen Levine, *Healing into Life and Death* (New York: Doubleday, Anchor Books, 1987), 37.

2. Langdon Gilkey, *Shantung Compound: The Story of Men and Women under Pressure* (New York: Harper & Row, 1966), 48.

3. Elie Wiesel, *Memoirs: All Rivers Run to the Sea* (New York: Schocken Books, 1995), 61.

4. Gilkey, *Shantung Compound*, 49.

5. Robert J. Landy, *Persona and Performance: The Meaning of Role in Drama, Therapy and Everyday Life* (New York: Guilford Press, 1993), 138–162, 247.

6. Louis A. Zurcher, *Social Roles: Conformity, Conflict, and Creativity* (Beverly Hills: Sage Publications, 1983), 53–56.

7. Julian Jaynes, *The Origin of Consciousness in the Breakdown of the Bicameral Mind* (Boston: Houghton Mifflin, 1976), 402.

8. Hannah Arendt, *The Life of the Mind* (Orlando, FL: Harcourt Brace Jovanovich, 1978), 30.

9. William James, "A Man's Social Self," in *The Principles of Psychology* (New York: Holt, 1893).

10. Nicholas Rescher, *Process Metaphysics: An Introduction to Process Philosophy* (Albany: State University of New York Press, 1996), 108.

Chapter 4: The Theatres of Society

1. Eric Bentley, *The Life of the Drama* (New York: Antheneum, 1967), 186.

2. Peter L. Berger, *The Precarious Vision: A Sociologist Looks at Social Fictions and Christian Faith* (New York: Doubleday, 1961), 25–26.

3. Ibid., 72.

4. Anne Lamott, *bird by bird* (New York: Doubleday, 1994), 34–35.

5. "Adam Smith," *The Money Game* (New York: Random House, 1967), 9–14.

6. Langdon Gilkey, *Shantung Compound: The Story of Men and Women under Pressure* (New York: Harper & Row, 1966), 26.

7. Ibid., 27.

8. Ibid.

9. Robert J. Landy, *Persona and Performance: The Meaning of Role in Drama, Therapy, and Everyday Life* (New York: Guilford Press, 1993), 6.

Chapter 5: Think, Don't Believe

1. Lillian Back and Merla Wolk, *Arenas of the Mind: Critical Reading for Writing* (New York: HarperCollins College Publishers, 1993), 382.

2. Eric Berne, M.D., *Games People Play: The Psychology of Human Relationships* (New York: Grove Press, 1964), 73–76.

3. Michael Talbot, *The Holographic Universe* (New York: HarperCollins, 1991), 25.

4. Robert E. Neale, *In Praise of Play: Toward a Psychology of Religion* (New York: Harper & Row, 1969), 39.

5. Stephen Levine, *Healing into Life and Death* (New York: Doubleday, Anchor Books, 1987), 7–8.

6. Berne, *Games People Play*, 160.

7. Nancy Mairs, "The Literature of Personal Disaster," in *The Best Writing on Writing*, ed. Jack Heffron (Cincinnati, OH: Story Press, F & W Publications, 1994), 65.

Chapter 6: Can Work Be Playful?

1. E. Mitchell and B. Mason, *The Theory of Play* (New York: A. S. Barnes, 1934), 88; quoted in *Play and Mental Health: Principles and Practice for Teachers*, John Eisele Davis (New York: A. S. Barnes, 1938), 146–147.

2. Susanna Millar, *The Psychology of Play* (Baltimore: Penguin Books, 1968), 21.

3. M. J. Ellis, *Why People Play* (Englewood Cliffs, NJ: Prentice-Hall, 1973), 21.

4. David L. Miller, *Gods and Games: Toward a Theology of Play* (New York: Harper Colophon Books, 1973), 174.

5. Paul R. Viotti and Mark V. Kauppi, *International Relations Theory: Realism, Pluralism, Globalism, and Beyond* (Boston: Allyn and Bacon, 1999), 204–207.

6. Lawrence P. Jacks, *Education through Recreation* (New York: Harper Bros., 1932), 39.

7. "Adam Smith," *The Money Game* (New York: Random, 1968), 10.

8. L. Casey Larijani, *The Virtual Reality Primer* (New York: McGraw-Hill, 1994), preface.

9. Ibid., 190.

10. Eric Berne, M.D., *Games People Play: The Psychology of Human Relationships* (New York: Grove Press, 1964), 23.

11. Stephen Minot, *Three Genres: The Writing of Poetry, Fiction, and Drama*, 6th ed. (Upper Saddle River, NJ: Prentice-Hall, 1998), 124.

12. Robert E. Neale, *In Praise of Play: Toward a Psychology of Religion* (New York: Harper & Row, 1969), 9.

13. Luther Halsey Gulick, *A Philosophy of Play* (Washington, DC: McGrath Publishing, 1920), 270–272.

14. Ibid.

15. Anthony D. Pellegrini, ed., *The Future of Play Theory: A Multidisciplinary Inquiry into the Contributions of Brian Sutton-Smith* (Albany: State University of New York Press, 1995), 213–214.

16. Ibid.

17. Lorrie Moore, "Better and Sicker," in *The Best Writing on Writing*, ed. Jack Heffron (Cincinnati, OH: Story Press, 1994), 187.

18. Adam Blatner, M.D. and Allee Blatner, *The Art of Play: An Adult's Guide to Reclaiming Imagination and Spontaneity* (New York: Human Sciences Press, 1988), 7.

Chapter 7: A Journey's Aim

1. Shri Nisragadatta Maharaj, *I Am That*, trans. Maurice Frydman (Durham, NC: Acorn Press, 1973), 95.

2. Morton Davis, *Game Theory: A Nontechnical Introduction*, rev. ed. (New York: Basic, 1983).

3. Cor Westland and Jane Knight, *Playing, Living, Learning: A Worldwide Perspective On Children's Opportunities to Play* (State College, PA: Venture Publishing, 1982), 9.

4. Elliot Aronson, *The Social Animal* (San Francisco: W. H. Freeman, 1976), 153.

5. Bertrand Russell, *The Conquest of Happiness* (New York: Horace Liveright, 1930), 45.

6. Alfie Kohn, "The Case Against Competition," in *Noetic Sciences Collection: 1980–1990, Ten Years of Consciousness Research* (Sausalito, CA: Noetic Sciences Institute, 1991), 90.

7. Ibid., 85.

8. Kohn, *No Contest: The Case against Competition* (Boston: Houghton, 1986), 9.

9. Ibid., 86.

10. Rollo May, *The Meaning of Anxiety*, rev. ed. (New York: W. W. Norton, 1977), foreword, 184–186.

11. Ibid., 112.

12. Karl Jaspers, *The Great Philosophers*, vol. 2 (Orlando, FL: Harcourt Brace, 1966), 333.

Chapter 8: Happiness and Bargains

1. Ervin Lszlo, *The Systems View of the World* (New York: George Braziller, 1972), 109.
2. William H. Rehnquist, "Successful Lawyers Pay the Price," *ABA Journal* (February 1996): 100.
3. Daniel Goleman, *Vital Lies—Simple Truths: The Psychology of Self-Deception* (New York: Simon & Schuster, 1985), 163–164.
4. "The Great Ideas: A Syntopicon," in *Great Books of the Western World*, (Chicago: Britannica, 1952) 1:684.
5. Elie Wiesel, *Memoirs: All Rivers Run to the Sea* (New York: Schocken Books, 1995), 116.
6. Susanna Millar, *The Psychology of Play* (Baltimore: Penguin Books, 1968), 184.
7. Gerry Spence, *From Freedom to Slavery* (New York: St. Martin's Press, 1993), 149–151.
8. Raphael Demos, "Spinoza's Doctrine of Privation," in *Studies in Spinoza: Critical and Interpretive Essays*, ed. S. Paul Kashap (Berkeley: University of California Press, 1972), 279–280.

Chapter 9: The War Game Nations Play

1. Alvin Toffler and Heidi Toffler, *War and Anti-War* (Boston: Little, Brown & Co., 1993), 13–14.
2. Charles W. Kegley Jr. and Eugene Wittkopf, eds., *American Foreign Policy: Pattern and Process*, 2d ed. (New York: St. Martin's Press, 1982), 279.
3. John E. Rielly, "Americans and the World: A Survey at Century's End," *Foreign Policy* (spring 1999): 100–102.
4. Donald Snow and Eugene Brown, *Beyond the Water's Edge: An Introduction to U.S. Foreign Policy* (New York: St. Martin's Press, 1997), 256.
5. Anthony D. Pellegrini, ed., *The Future of Play Theory: A Multidisciplinary Inquiry into the Contributions of Brian Sutton-Smith* (Albany: State University of New York Press, 1995), 213.
6. Joseph S. Nye Jr., *Understanding International Conflicts: An Introduction to Theory and History* (New York: HarperCollins College Publications, 1993), 181.
7. Robley Wilson, "War," in *Three Genres*, Minot, 20.
8. Deb Mulvey and Clancy Strock, eds., *We Pulled Together... And Won!* (Greendale, WI: Reiman Publications, 1993), prologue, 8.
9. Ibid., 90.
10. Ibid., 68.

11. Henry Steele Commager, ed., *The Blue and the Gray: The Story of the Civil War as Told by Participants* (New York: Fairfax Press, 1982), introduction.
12. Ibid., 53.
13. Ibid., 107–108.
14. Alan Cassels, *Ideology and International Relations in the Modern World* (New York: Routledge, 1996), 18.
15. "The Great Ideas: A Syntopicon," in *Great Books of the Western World*, (Chicago: Britannica, 1952), 2:1013.
16. Ibid.
17. Ronald Steel, "The Domestic Core of Foreign Policy," in *The Domestic Sources of American Foreign Policy*, eds. Eugene Wittkopf and James McCormick, 3rd ed. (Lanham, MD: Rowman & Littlefield, 1999), 32.
18. John W. Loy and Graham L. Hesheth, "Competitive Play on the Plains: An Analysis of Games and Warfare among Native American Warrior Societies," in *The Future of Play Theory*, ed. Anthony D. Pellegrini (Albany: State University of New York Press, 1995), 76.
19. Ibid., 80–81.
20. Steven Metz, "Racing Toward the Future: The Revolution in Military Affairs," in *The Future of American Foreign Policy*, eds. Eugene Wittkopf and Christopher Jones (New York: St. Martin's/Worth, 1999), 315–318. (Reprinted from *Current History Magazine*, April 1997.)
21. Will Durant, *The Story of Civilization, Part II* (New York: Simon & Schuster, 1975), 249.
22. Alfred North Whitehead, *Adventures of Ideas* (New York: Simon & Schuster, Free Press, 1967), 6.
23. Karl Von Clausewitz, *What Is War?* in *Encyclopedia Britannica: Gateway*, 7:494.
24. Robert E. Neale, *In Praise of Play: Toward a Psychology of Religion* (New York: Harper & Row, 1969), 44.
25. Michael J. Apter, *The Dangerous Edge: The Psychology of Excitement* (New York: Free Press, 1992), 3.
26. Snow and Brown, *Beyond the Water's Edge*, 133.
27. Whitehead, *Adventures of Ideas*, 32.
28. *Einstein on Peace*, eds. Otto Nathan and Heinz Norden (New York: Random House, Schocken Books, 1960), 3–4.
29. Pellegrini, *Future of Play Theory*, 25.
30. Toffler, *War and Anti-War*, 15.
31. Nathan and Norden, *Einstein on Peace*, 136.
32. Toffler, *War and Anti-War*, 10–11.
33. Warren Christopher, "Force, Diplomacy, and the Resources We Need for American Leadership," *U.S. Department of State Dispatch*, 28 October 1996, vol. 7, no. 44, 533 (3).

Chapter 10: Peace Dance in the Moonlight

1. Ron J. Flemming, *Heartbeats: A Book of Wisdom* (Hanover, MA: Christopher Publishing House, 1994), 2.
2. Robert E. Neale, *In Praise of Play: Toward a Psychology of Religion* (New York: Harper & Row, 1969), 46.
3. David Flusser and Carol Glucker, trans., *The Spiritual History of the Dead Sea Sect* (Tel Aviv: MOD, 1989), 28.
4. M. K. Gandhi, *Non-Violence in Peace and War* (Ahmedabad, India: Navajivan Publishing House, 1948).

Chapter 11: Theories of Play and Healing: Reviewing Research

1. Michael J. Ellis, *Why People Play* (Englewood Cliffs, NJ: Prentice-Hall, 1973), 23–48.
2. Robert E. Neale, *In Praise of Play: Toward a Psychology of Religion* (New York: Harper & Row, 1969), 22–23.
3. Ibid., 24.
4. Ellis, *Why People Play*, 77–79.
5. Anthony D. Pellegrini, ed., *The Future of Play Theory: A Multidisciplinary Inquiry into the Contributions of Brian Sutton-Smith* (Albany: State University of New York Press, 1995), 282.
6. Susanna Millar, *The Psychology of Play* (Baltimore: Penguin Books, 1968), 179.
7. Ibid., 192–193.
8. Robert J. Landy, *Persona and Performance: The Meaning of Role in Drama, Therapy, and Everyday Life* (New York: Guilford Press, 1993), 56–110.
9. Ibid., 12.
10. Ibid., 111–121.
11. Lillian Back and Merla Wolk, *Arenas of the Mind: Critical Reading for Writing* (New York: HarperCollins College Publishers, 1993), 458–459.
12. Hugo Rahner, *Man at Play* (New York: Herder & Herder, 1972), 39.
13. F. A. Beach, *Current Concepts of Play in Animals*, quoted in *Psychology of Play*, Millar, 59.
14. W. H. Thorpe, *Learning and Instinct in Animals* (London: Methuen, 1963), 363.
15. Millar, *Psychology of Play*, 81.
16. Ibid., 94.
17. Jeffrey Moussaieff Masson and Susan McCarthy, *When Elephants Weep: The Emotional Lives of Animals* (New York: Dell Publishing, Delta Book, 1995), 111–132.
18. Millar, *Psychology of Play*, 61.

19. Masson and McCarthy, *When Elephants Weep*, 118.
20. Ibid., 112.

Chapter 12: Life Is Tough, Tough But Fun

1. Robert E. Neale, *In Praise of Play: Toward a Psychology of Religion* (New York: Harper & Row, 1969), 173.
2. Anna K. Nardo, "The Poetry of John Donne's Lomonal Play," in *The Paradoxes of Play: Proceedings of the Sixth Annual Meeting of the Association for the Anthropological Study of Play*, ed. John W. Loy (West Point, NY: Leisure Press, 1982), 38.
3. Susanna Millar, *The Psychology of Play* (Baltimore: Penguin Books, 1968), 155.
4. Hugo Rahner, *Man at Play* (New York: Herder & Herder, 1972), 30–31.
5. David L. Miller, *Gods and Games: Toward a Theology of Play* (New York: Harper & Row, Harper Colophon Books, 1973), 91–92.
6. Joshua Liebman, *Peace of Mind* (New York: Simon & Schuster, 1946), 135.

Epilogue

1. Hugo Rahner, *Man at Play* (New York: Herder & Herder, 1972), 7–8.

Bibliography

Play Theory

Berne, Eric, M.D. *Games People Play: The Psychology of Human Relationships.* New York: Grove Press, 1964.

Birenbaum, Arnold, and Edward Sagarin, eds. *People in Places: The Sociology of the Familiar.* New York: Praeger Publishers, 1973.

Blatner, Adam, M.D., and Allee Blatner. *The Art of Play: An Adult's Guide to Reclaiming Imagination and Spontaneity.* New York: Human Sciences Press, 1988.

Caplan, Frank, and Theresa Caplan. *The Power of Play.* Garden City, NY: Doubleday, Anchor Books, 1973.

Davis, John Eisele. *Play and Mental Health: Principles and Practice for Teachers.* New York: A. S. Barnes, 1938.

Davis, Morton. *Game Theory: A Nontechnical Introduction,* rev. ed. New York: Basic Books, 1983.

Ellis, M. J. *Why People Play.* Englewood Cliffs, NJ: Prentice-Hall, 1973.

Gulick, Luther Halsey, M.D. *A Philosophy of Play.* Washington, DC: McGrath Publishing, 1920.

Huizinga, Johan. *Homo Ludens: A Study of the Play Element in Culture.* Boston: Beacon Press, 1955.

Lancy, David F., and B. Allan Tindall, eds. *The Anthropological Study of Play: Problems and Prospects, Proceedings of the First Annual Meeting of the Association for the Anthropological Study of Play.* Cornwall, NY: Leisure Press, 1976.

Landy, Robert J. *Persona and Performance: The Meaning of Role in Drama, Therapy, and Everyday Life.* New York: Guilford Press, 1993.

Lehman, Harvey C., and Paul A. Witty. *The Psychology of Play Activities.* New York: A. S. Barnes, 1927. Reprint, New York: Arno Press, 1976.

Loy, John W., ed. *The Paradoxes of Play: Proceedings of the Sixth Annual Meeting of the Association for the Anthropological Study of Play.* West Point, NY: Leisure Press, 1982.
Millar, Susanna. *The Psychology of Play.* Baltimore: Penguin Books, 1968.
Miller, David L. *Gods and Games: Toward a Theology of Play.* New York: Harper Colophon Books, 1973.
Neale, Robert E. *In Praise of Play: Toward a Psychology of Religion.* New York: Harper & Row, 1969.
Pellegrini, Anthony D., ed. *The Future of Play Theory: A Multidisciplinary Inquiry into the Contributions of Brian Sutton-Smith.* Albany: State University of New York Press, 1995.
Rahner, Hugo. *Man at Play.* New York: Herder & Herder, 1972.
Sapora, Allen V., and Elmer D. Mitchell. *The Theory of Play and Recreation,* 3rd ed. New York: Ronald Press, 1961.
Scheff, T. J. *Catharsis in Healing, Ritual, and Drama.* Berkeley: University of California Press, 1979.
Slovenko, Ralph, and James A. Knight, eds. *Motivations in Play, Games, and Sports.* Springfield, IL: Charles C. Thomas Publishing, 1967.
Westland, Cor, and Jane Knight. *Playing, Living, Learning: A Worldwide Perspective on Children's Opportunities to Play.* State College, PA: Venture Publishing, 1982.
Winnicott, D. W. *Playing and Reality.* New York: Basic Books, 1971.
Zurcher, Louis A. *Social Roles: Conformity, Conflict, and Creativity.* Beverly Hills: Sage Publications, 1983.

Philosophy, Psychology, and Social Sciences

Berger, Peter L. *The Precarious Vision: A Sociologist Looks at Social Fictions and Christian Faith.* New York: Doubleday, 1961.
———, and Thomas Luckmann. *The Social Construction of Reality: A Treatise in the Sociology of Knowledge.* Garden City, NY: Doubleday, 1966.
Brenner, Paul [Alex Voyd, pseud.], *Dear Brotherhood: A Fantasy.* Ashland, OR: School of Life Publications, 1995.
Dossey, Larry, M.D. *Healing Words: The Power of Prayer and the Practice of Medicine.* New York: HarperCollins, 1993.
Einstein, Albert. *Out of My Later Years.* rev. reprinted ed. Westport: Greenwood Press, 1970.
Fromm, Eric. *The Anatomy of Human Destructiveness.* New York: Holt, Rinehart & Winston, 1973.
Gilkey, Langdon. *Shantung Compound: The Story of Men and Women under Pressure.* New York: Harper & Row, 1966.
Goleman, Daniel. *Vital Lies—Simple Truths: The Psychology of Self-Deception.* New York: Simon & Schuster, 1985.

Jaynes, Julian. *The Origin of Consciousness in the Breakdown of the Bicameral Mind*. Boston: Houghton Mifflin, 1976.
Kegley, Charles W., Jr., and Eugene R. Wittkopf, eds. *American Foreign Policy: Pattern and Process*, 2d ed. New York: St. Martin's Press, 1982.
Kohn, Alfie. *No Contest: The Case against Competition*. Boston: Houghton Mifflin, 1986.
Lamott, Anne. *bird by bird*. New York: Doubleday, 1994.
Levine, Stephen. *Healing into Life and Death*. New York: Doubleday, Anchor Books, 1987.
Lowe, Victor. *Understanding Whitehead*. Baltimore: Johns Hopkins Press, 1962.
Masson, Jeffrey Moussaieff, and Susan McCarthy. *When Elephants Weep: The Emotional Lives of Animals*. New York: Dell Publishing, Delta Book, 1995.
Quinn, Daniel. *Ishmael*. New York: Bantam Doubleday Dell Publishing, Bantam Books, 1992.
Rescher, Nicholas. *Process Metaphysics: An Introduction to Process Philosophy*. Albany: State University of New York Press, 1996.
Rosten, Leo. *The Joys of Yiddish*. New York: Pocket Books, 1968.
Santayana, George. *Skepticism and Animal Faith: An Introduction to a System of Philosophy*. New York: Dover Publications, 1955.
"Smith, Adam." *The Money Game*. New York: Random, 1967.
Snow, Donald, and Eugene Brown. *Beyond the Water's Edge: An Introduction to U.S. Foreign Policy*. New York: St. Martin's Press, 1997.
Spinoza, Baruch Benedict. *The Ethics*. Trans. R. H. M. Elwes. New York: Dover Publications, 1955.
Stark, Rodney, and William Sims Bainbridge. *The Future of Religion: Secularization, Revival, and Cult Formation*. Berkeley: University of California Press, 1985.
Toffler, Alvin, and Heidi Toffler. *War and Anti-War*. Boston: Little, Brown & Company, 1993.
Von Neumann, John, and Oskar Morgentern. *The Theory of Games and Economic Behavior*. Princeton, NJ: Princeton University Press, 1980.
Whitehead, Alfred North. *Adventures of Ideas*. New York: Simon & Schuster, Free Press, 1967.
Wiesel, Elie. *Memoirs: All Rivers Run to the Sea*. New York: Schocken Books, 1995.
Wittkopf, Eugene R., and James McCormick, eds. *The Domestic Sources of American Foreign Policy: Insights and Evidence*, 3rd ed. Lanham, MD: Rowman & Littlefield, 1999.

www.ingramcontent.com/pod-product-compliance
Lightning Source LLC
Chambersburg PA
CBHW020802160426
43192CB00006B/403